The Writing of Fiction

Edith Wharton

A TOUCHSTONE BOOK
Published by Simon & Schuster

To Gaillard Lapsley

TOUCHSTONE
Rockefeller Center
1230 Avenue of the Americas
New York, NY 10020

First Touchstone Edition 1997

TOUCHSTONE and colophon are registered trademarks
of Simon & Schuster Inc.

Designed by Judy Wong

Manufactured in the United States of America

1   3   5   7   9   10   8   6   4   2

Library of Congress Cataloging-in-Publication Data
Wharton, Edith, 1862–1937.
The writing of fiction / Edith Wharton.
p.   cm.
"A Touchstone book."
Originally published: New York ; London : C. Scribner, 1925.
1. Fiction—Authorship. 2. Creative writing. I. Title.
PN3355.W5 1997
808.3—dc21   97-14791
CIP

ISBN 0-684-84531-8

I

In General

I

In General

I

To treat of the practice of fiction is to deal with the newest, most fluid and least formulated of the arts. The exploration of origins is always fascinating; but the attempt to relate the modern novel to the tale of Joseph and his Brethren is of purely historic interest.

Modern fiction really began when the "action" of the novel was transferred from the street to the soul; and this step was probably first taken when Madame de La Fayette, in the seventeenth century, wrote a little story called "La Princesse de Clèves," a story of hopeless love and mute renunciation in which the stately tenor of the lives depicted is hardly ruffled by the exultations and agonies succeeding each other below the surface.

The next advance was made when the protagonists of this new inner drama were transformed from conventionalized puppets—the hero, the heroine, the villain, the heavy father and so on—into breathing and recognizable human beings. Here again a French novelist—the Abbé Prévost—led the way with "Manon Lescaut"; but his drawing of character seems summary and schematic when his people are compared with the first great figure in modern fiction—the appalling "Neveu de Rameau." It was not till long after Diderot's death that the author of so many brilliant tales peopled with eighteenth century puppets was found, in the creation of that one sordid, cynical and desolately human figure, to have anticipated not only Balzac but Dostoievsky.

But even from "Manon Lescaut" and the "Neveu de Rameau," even from Lesage, Defoe, Fielding, Smollett, Richardson, and Scott, modern fiction is differentiated by the great dividing geniuses of Balzac and Stendhal. Save for that one amazing accident of Diderot's, Balzac was the first not only to see his people, physically and morally, in their habit as they lived, with all their personal hobbies and infirmities, and make the reader see them, but to draw his dramatic action as much from the relation of his characters to their houses, streets, towns, professions, inherited habits and opinions, as from their fortuitous contacts with each other.

Balzac himself ascribed the priority in this kind of realism to Scott, from whom the younger novelist avowedly derived his chief inspiration. But, as Balzac observed, Scott, so keen and direct in surveying the rest of his field of vision, became conventional and hypocritical when he touched on love and women. In deference to the wave of prudery which overswept England after the vulgar excesses of the Hanoverian court he substituted sentimentality for passion, and reduced his heroines to "Keepsake" insipidities; whereas in the firm surface of Balzac's realism there is hardly a flaw, and his women, the young as well as the old, are living people, as much compact of human contradictions and torn with human passions as his misers, his financiers, his priests or his doctors.

Stendhal, though as indifferent as any eighteenth century writer to atmosphere and "local colour," is intensely modern and realistic in the individualizing of his characters, who were never types (to the extent even of some of Balzac's) but always sharply differentiated and particular human beings. More distinctively still does he represent the new fiction by his insight into the springs of social action. No modern novelist has ever gone nearer than Racine did in his tragedies to the sources of personal, of individual feeling; and some of the French novelists of the eighteenth century are still unsurpassed (save by Racine) in the last refinements of individual soul-analysis. What was new in both Balzac and Stendhal was the fact of their viewing each character first of all as a product of particular material and social conditions, as being thus or thus because of the calling he pursued or the house he lived in (Balzac), or the society he wanted to get into (Stendhal), or the acre of ground he coveted, or the powerful or fashionable personage he aped or envied (both Balzac and Stendhal). These novelists (with the solitary exception of

Defoe, when he wrote "Moll Flanders") are the first to seem continuously aware that the bounds of a personality are not reproducible by a sharp black line, but that each of us flows imperceptibly into adjacent people and things.

The characterization of all the novelists who preceded these two masters seems, in comparison, incomplete or immature. Even Richardson's seems so, in the most penetrating pages of "Clarissa Harlowe," even Goethe's in that uncannily modern novel, the "Elective Affinities"—because, in the case of these writers, the people so elaborately dissected are hung in the void, unvisualized and unconditioned (or almost) by the special outward circumstances of their lives. They are subtly analyzed abstractions of humanity, to whom only such things happen as might happen to almost any one in any walk of life—the inevitable eternal human happenings.

Since Balzac and Stendhal, fiction has reached out in many new directions, and made all sorts of experiments; but it has never ceased to cultivate the ground they cleared for it, or gone back to the realm of abstractions. It is still, however, an art in the making, fluent and dirigible, and combining a past full enough for the deduction of certain general principles with a future rich in untried possibilities.

II

On the threshold of any theory of art its exponent is sure to be asked: "On what first assumption does your theory rest?" And in fiction, as in every other art, the only answer seems to be that any theory must begin by assuming the need of selection. It seems curious that even now—and perhaps more than ever—one should have to explain and defend what is no more than the rule underlying the most artless verbal statement. No matter how restricted an incident one is trying to give an account of, it cannot but be fringed with details more and more remotely relevant, and beyond that with an outer mass of irrelevant facts which may crowd on the narrator simply because of some accidental propinquity in time or space. To choose between all this material is the first step toward coherent expression.

A generation ago this was so generally taken for granted that to state it would have seemed pedantic. In every-day intercourse the principle survives in the injunction to stick to the point; but the novelist who applies—or owns up to applying—this rule to his art, is nowadays accused of being absorbed in technique to the exclusion of the supposedly contrary element of "human interest."

Even now, the charge would hardly be worth taking up had it not lately helped to refurbish the old trick of the early French "realists," that group of brilliant writers who invented the once-famous *tranche de vie*, the exact photographic reproduction of a situation or an episode, with all its sounds, smells, aspects realistically rendered, but with its deeper relevance and its suggestions of a larger whole either unconsciously missed or purposely left out. Now that half a century has elapsed, one sees that those among this group of writers who survive are still readable in spite of their constricting theory, or in proportion as they forgot about it once they closed with their subject. Such are Maupassant, who packed into his brief masterpieces so deep a psychological significance and so sure a sense of larger relations; Zola, whose "slices" became the stuff of great romantic allegories in which the forces of Nature and Industry are the huge cloudy protagonists, as in a Pilgrim's Progress of man's material activities; and the Goncourts, whose French instinct for psychological analysis always made them seize on the more significant morsel of the famous slices. As for the pupils, the mere conscientious appliers of the system, they have all blown away with the theory, after a briefer popularity than writers of equal talent might have enjoyed had they not thus narrowed their scope. An instance in proof is Feydeau's "Fanny," one of the few "psychological" novels of that generation, and a slight enough adventure in soul-searching compared with the great "Madame Bovary" (which it was supposed at the time to surpass), but still readable enough to have kept the author's name alive, while most of his minor contemporaries are buried under the unappetizing *débris* of their "slices."

It seemed necessary to revert to the slice of life because it has lately reappeared, marked by certain unimportant differences, and relabelled the stream of consciousness;

and, curiously enough, without its new exponents' appearing aware that they are not also its originators. This time the theory seems to have sprung up first in England and America; but it has already spread to certain of the younger French novelists, who are just now, confusedly if admiringly, rather overconscious of recent tendencies in English and American fiction.

The stream of consciousness method differs from the slice of life in noting mental as well as visual reactions, but resembles it in setting them down just as they come, with a deliberate disregard of their relevance in the particular case, or rather with the assumption that their very unsorted abundance constitutes in itself the author's subject.

This attempt to note down every half-aware stirring of thought and sensation, the automatic reactions to every passing impression, is not as new as its present exponents appear to think. It has been used by most of the greatest novelists, not as an end in itself, but as it happened to serve their general design: as when their object was to portray a mind in one of those moments of acute mental stress when it records with meaningless precision a series of disconnected impressions. The value of such "effects" in making vivid a tidal rush of emotion has never been unknown since fiction became psychological, and novelists grew aware of the intensity with which, at such times, irrelevant trifles impinge upon the brain; but they have never been deluded by the idea that the subconscious—that Mrs. Harris of the psychologists—could in itself furnish the materials for their art. All the greatest of them, from Balzac and Thackeray onward, have made use of the stammerings and mur-murings of the half-conscious mind whenever—but only when—such a state of mental flux fitted into the whole picture of the person portrayed. Their observation showed them that in the world of normal men life is conducted, at least in its decisive moments, on fairly coherent and selective lines, and that only thus can the great fundamental affairs of bread-getting and home-and-tribe organizing be carried on. Drama, situation, is made out of the conflicts thus produced between social order and individual appetites, and the art of rendering life in fiction can never, in the last analysis, be anything, or need to be anything, but the disengaging of crucial moments from the welter of existence. These moments need not involve action in the sense of external events; they seldom have, since the scene of conflict was shifted from incident to character. But there must be something that *makes* them crucial, some recognizable relation to a familiar social or moral standard, some explicit aware-ness of the eternal struggle between man's contending impulses, if the tales embodying them are to fix the attention and hold the memory.

III

The distrust of technique and the fear of being unoriginal—both symptoms of a certain lack of creative abundance—are in truth leading to pure anarchy in fiction, and one is almost tempted to say that in certain schools formlessness is now regarded as the first condition of form.

Not long ago I heard a man of letters declare that Dostoievsky was superior to Tolstoy because his mind was "more chaotic," and he could therefore render more "truthfully" the chaos of the Russian mind in general; though how chaos can be apprehended and defined by a mind immersed in it, the speaker did not make clear. The assertion, of course, was the result of confusing imaginative emotivity with its objective rendering. What the speaker meant was that the novelist who would create a given group of people or portray special social conditions must be able to identify himself with them; which is rather a long way of saying that an artist must have imagination.

The chief difference between the merely sympathetic and the creative imagination is that the latter is two-sided, and combines with the power of penetrating into other minds that of standing far enough aloof from them to see beyond, and relate them to the whole stuff of life out of which they but partially emerge. Such an all-round view can be obtained only by mounting to a height; and that height, in art, is proportioned to the artist's power of detaching one part of his imagination from the particular problem in which the rest is steeped.

One of the causes of the confusion of judgment on this point is no doubt the perilous affinity between the art of fiction and the material it works in. It has been so often said that all art is re-presentation—the giving back in conscious form of the shapeless raw material of experience—that one would willingly avoid insisting on such a truism. But while there is no art of which the saying is truer than of fiction, there is none in respect of which there is more danger of the axiom's being misinterpreted. The attempt to give back any fragment of life in painting or sculpture or music presupposes transposition, "stylization." To re-present in words is far more difficult, because the relation is so close between model and artist. The novelist works in the very material out of which the object he is trying to render is made. He must use, to express soul, the signs which soul uses to express itself. It is relatively easy to separate the artistic vision of an object from its complex and tangled actuality if one has to re-see it in paint or marble or bronze; it is infinitely difficult to render a human mind when one is employing the very word-dust with which thought is formulated.

Still, the transposition does take place as surely, if not as obviously, in a novel as in a statue. If it did not, the writing of fiction could never be classed among works of art, products of conscious ordering and selecting, and there would consequently be nothing to say about it, since there seems to be no way of estimating æsthetically anything to which no standard of choice can be applied.

Another unsettling element in modern art is that common symptom of immaturity, the dread of doing what has been done before; for though one of the instincts of youth is imitation, another, equally imperious, is that of fiercely guarding against it. In this respect, the novelist of the present day is in danger of being caught in a vicious circle, for the insatiable demand for quick production tends to keep him in a state of perpetual immaturity, and the ready acceptance of his wares encourages him to think that no time need be wasted in studying the past history of his art, or in speculating on its principles. This conviction strengthens the belief that the so-called quality of "originality" may be impaired by too long brooding on one's theme and too close a commerce with the past; but the whole history of that past—in every domain of art—disproves this by what survives, and shows that every subject, to yield and to retain its full flavour, should be long carried in the mind, brooded upon, and fed with all the impressions and emotions which nourish its creator.

True originality consists not in a new manner but in a new vision. That new, that personal, vision is attained only by looking long enough at the object represented to make it the writer's own; and the mind which would bring this secret germ to fruition must be able to nourish it with an accumulated wealth of knowledge and experience. To know any one thing one must not only know something of a great many others, but also, as Matthew Arnold long since pointed out, a great deal more of one's immediate subject than any partial presentation of it visibly includes; and Mr. Kipling's "What should they know of England who only England know?" might be taken as the symbolic watchword of the creative artist.

One is sometimes tempted to think that the generation which has invented the "fiction course" is getting the fiction it deserves. At any rate it is fostering in its young writers the conviction that art is neither long nor arduous, and perhaps blinding them to the fact that notoriety and mediocrity are often interchangeable terms. But though the trade-wind in fiction undoubtedly drives many beginners along the line of least resistance, and holds them there, it is far from being the sole cause of the present quest for short-cuts in art. There are writers indifferent to popular success, and even contemptuous of it, who sincerely believe that this line marks the path of the true vocation. Many people assume that the artist receives, at the outset of his career, the mysterious sealed orders known as "Inspiration," and has only to let that sovereign impulse carry him where it will. Inspiration does indeed come at the outset to every creator, but it comes most often as an infant, helpless, stumbling, inarticulate, to be taught and guided; and the beginner, during this time of training his gift, is as likely to misuse it as a young parent to make mistakes in teaching his first child.

There is no doubt that in this day of general "speeding up," the "inspirational" theory is seductive even to those who care nothing for easy triumphs. No writer—especially at the beginning of his career—can help being influenced by the quality of the audience that awaits him; and the young novelist may ask of what use are experience and meditation, when his readers are so incapable of giving him either. The answer is that he will never do his best till he ceases altogether to think of his readers (and his editor and his publisher) and begins to write, not for himself, but for that *other self* with whom the creative artist is always in mysterious correspondence, and who, happily, has an objective existence somewhere, and will some day receive the message sent to him, though the sender may never know it. As to experience, intellectual and moral, the creative imagination can make a little go a long way, provided it remains long enough in the mind and is sufficiently brooded upon. One good heart-break will furnish the poet with many songs, and the novelist with a considerable number of novels. But they must have hearts that can break.

Even to the writer least concerned with popularity it is difficult, at first, to defend his personality. Study and meditation contain their own perils. Counsellors intervene with contradictory advice and instances. In such cases these counsellors are most often other people's novels: the great novels of the past, which haunt the beginner like a passion, and the works of his contemporaries, which pull him this way and that with too-persuasive hands. His impulse, at first, will be either to shun them, to his own impoverishment, or to let his dawning individuality be lost in theirs; but gradually he will come to see that he must learn to listen to them, take all they can give, absorb it into himself, and then turn to his own task with the fixed resolve to see life only through his own eyes.

Even then another difficulty remains; the mysterious discrepancy which sometimes exists between a novelist's vision of life and his particular kind of talent. Not infrequently an innate tendency to see things in large masses is combined with the technical inability to render them otherwise than separately, meticulously, on a small scale. Perhaps more failures than one is aware of are due to this particular lack of proportion between the powers of vision and expression. At any rate, it is the cause of some painful struggles and arid dissatisfactions; and the only remedy is resolutely to abandon the larger for the smaller field, to narrow one's vision to one's pencil, and do the small thing closely and deeply rather than the big thing loosely and superficially. Of twenty subjects that tempt the imagination (subjects one sees one's self doing, oh so wonderfully, if only one were Mérimée or Maupassant, or Conrad or Mr. Kipling!) probably but one is "fit for the hand" of the limited person one happens to be; and to learn to renounce the others is a first step toward doing that particular one well.

IV

These considerations have led straight to the great, the central, matter of subject; and inextricably interwoven with it are the subsidiary points of form and style, both of which ought, as it were, to spring naturally out of the particular theme chosen for representation.

Form might perhaps, for present purposes, be defined as the order, in time and importance, in which the incidents of the narrative are grouped; and style as the way in which they are presented, not only in the narrower sense of language, but also, and rather, as they are grasped and coloured by their medium, the narrator's mind, and given back in his words. It is the quality of the medium which gives these incidents their quality; style, in this sense, is the most personal ingredient in the combination of things out of which any work of art is made. Words are the exterior symbols of thought, and it is only by their exact use that the writer can keep on his subject the close and patient hold which "fishes the murex up," and steeps his creation in unfading colours.

Style in this definition is discipline; and the self-consecration it demands, and the bearing it has on the whole of the artist's effort, have been admirably summed up by Marcel Proust in that searching chapter of "A l'Ombre des Jeunes Filles en Fleurs" where he analyzes the art of fiction in the person of the great novelist Bergotte. "The severity of his taste, his unwillingness to write anything of which he could not say, in his favourite phrase: *'C'est doux'* [harmonious, delicious], this determination, which had caused him to spend so many seemingly fruitless years in the 'precious' carving of trifles, was in reality the secret of his strength; for habit makes the style of the writer as it makes the character of the man, and the author who has several times contented himself with expressing his thought in an approximately pleasing way *has once and for all set a boundary to his talent, and will never pass beyond."*

These definitions of form and style being established, and the preliminary need of the harmony between an author's talent and his argument being assumed, one is next faced by the profounder problem of the inherent fitness of any given subject as material for the imagination.

It has been often said that subject in itself is all-important, and at least as often that it is of no importance whatever. Definition is again necessary before the truth can be extracted from these contradictions. Subject, obviously, is *what the story is about;* but whatever the central episode or situation chosen by the novelist, his tale will be about only just so much of it as he reacts to. A gold mine is worth nothing unless the owner has the machinery for extracting the ore, and each subject must be considered first in itself, and next in relation to the novelist's power of extracting from it what it contains. There are subjects trivial in appearance, and subjects trivial to the core; and the novelist ought to be able to discern at a glance between the two, and know in which case it is worth while to set about sinking his shaft. But the novelist may make mistakes. He is exposed to the temptation of the false good-subject, and learns only by prolonged experience to resist surface-attractions, and probe his story to the depths before he begins to tell it.

There is still another way in which subject must be tested. Any subject considered in itself must first of all respond in some way to that mysterious need of a judgment on life of which the most detached human intellect, provided it be a normal one, cannot, apparently, rid itself. Whether the "moral" be present in the guise of the hero rescuing the heroine from the villain at the point of the revolver, or whether it lurk in the quiet irony of such a scene as Pendennis's visit to the Grey Friars' Chapel, and his hearing the choir singing "I have been young, and now am old; yet have I not seen the righteous forsaken, nor his seed begging their bread," at the very moment when he discovers the bent head of Colonel Newcome among the pauper gentlemen—in one form or another there must be some sort of rational response to the reader's unconscious but insistent inner question: "What am I being told this story for? What judgment on life does it contain for me?"

There seems to be no escape from this obligation except into a pathological world where the action, taking place between people of abnormal psychology, and not keeping time with our normal human rhythms, becomes an idiot's tale, signifying nothing. In vain has it been attempted to set up a water-tight compartment between "art" and "morality." All the great novelists whose books have been used to point the argument have invariably declared themselves on the other side, not only by the inner significance of their work, but also, in some cases, by the most explicit statements. Flaubert, for instance, so often cited as the example of the writer viewing his themes in a purely "scientific" or amoral light, has disproved the claim by providing the other camp with that perfect formula: *"Plus la pensée est belle, plus la phrase est sonore"*—not the metaphor, not the picture, but *the thought*.

A good subject, then, must contain in itself something that sheds a light on our moral experience. If it is incapable of this expansion, this vital radiation, it remains, however showy a surface it presents, a mere irrelevant happening, a meaningless scrap of fact torn out of its context. Nor is it more than a half-truth to say that the imagination which probes deep enough can find this germ in any happening, however insignificant. The converse is true enough: the limited imagination reduces a great theme to its own measure. But the wide creative vision, though no fragment of human experience can appear wholly empty to it, yet seeks by instinct those subjects in which some phase of our common plight stands forth dramatically and typically, subjects which, in themselves, are a kind of summary or foreshortening of life's dispersed and inconclusive occurrences.

II

Telling a Short Story

II

Telling a Short Story

I

Like the modern novel, the modern short story seems to have originated—or at least received its present stamp—in France. English writers, in this line, were slower in attaining the point to which the French and Russians first carried the art.

Since then the short story has developed, and reached out in fresh directions, in the hands of such novelists as Mr. Hardy (only occasionally at his best in this form), of Stevenson, James, and Conrad, all three almost unfailingly excellent in it, of Mr. Kipling, past-master of the *conte,* and Sir Arthur Quiller-Couch, whose delightful early volumes, "Noughts and Crosses" and "I Saw Three Ships," are less known than they deserve to be. These writers had long been preceded by Scott in "Wandering

Willy's Tale" and other short stories, by Poe, the sporadic and unaccountable, and by Hawthorne; but almost all the best tales of Scott, Hawthorne, and Poe belong to that peculiar category of the eerie which lies outside of the classic tradition.

When the novel of manners comes to be dealt with, classification in order of time will have to be reversed, and in order of merit will be less easy; for even against Balzac, Tolstoy, and Turgenev the genius of the great English observers, from Richardson and Jane Austen to Thackeray and Dickens, will weigh heavily in the balance. With regard to the short story, however, and especially to that compactest form of it, the short short-story or *conte,* its first specimens are undoubtedly of continental production; but happily for English letters the generation who took over and adapted the formula were nursed on the Goethean principle that "those who remain imprisoned in the false notion of their own originality will always fall short of what they might have accomplished."

The sense of form—already defined as the order, in time and importance, in which the narrated incidents are grouped—is, in all the arts, specifically of the classic, the Latin tradition. A thousand years of form (in the widest disciplinary sense), of its observance, its application, its tacit acceptance as the first condition of artistic expression, have cleared the ground, for the French writer of fiction, of many superfluous encumbrances. As the soil of France is of all soils the most weeded, tilled, and ductile, so the field of art, wherever French culture

TELLING A SHORT STORY

extends, is the most worked-over and the most prepared for whatever seed is to be sown in it.

But when the great Russians (who owe to French culture much more than is generally conceded) took over that neat thing, the French *nouvelle,* they gave it the additional dimension it most often lacked. In any really good subject one has only to probe deep enough to come to tears; and the Russians almost always dig to that depth. The result has been to give to the short story, as French and Russian art have combined to shape it, great closeness of texture with profundity of form. Instead of a loose web spread over the surface of life they have made it, at its best, a shaft driven straight into the heart of human experience.

II

Though the critic no longer feels that need of classifying and sub-classifying the *genres* which so preoccupied the contemporaries of Wordsworth, there are, in all the arts, certain local products that seem to necessitate a parenthesis.

Such, in fiction, is the use of the supernatural. It seems to have come from mysterious Germanic and Armorican forests, from lands of long twilights and wailing winds; and it certainly did not pass through French or even Russian hands to reach us. Sorcerers and magic are of the south, the Mediterranean; the witch of Theocritus brewed a brew fit for her sister-hags of the Scottish heath; but the spectral apparition walks only in the pages of English and Germanic fiction.

It has done so, to great effect, in some of the most original of our great English short stories, from Scott's "Wandering Willy" and Poe's awful hallucinations to Le Fanu's "Watcher," and from the "Thrawn Janet" of Stevenson to "The Turn of the Screw" of Henry James, last great master of the eerie in English.

All these tales, in which the effect sought is completely achieved, are models of the subtlest artifice. It is not enough to believe in ghosts, or even to have seen one, to be able to write a good ghost story. The greater the improbability to be overcome the more studied must be the approach, the more perfectly maintained the air of naturalness, the easy assumption that things are always likely to happen in that way.

One of the chief obligations, in a short story, is to give the reader an immediate sense of security. Every phrase should be a sign-post, and never (unless intentionally) a misleading one: the reader must feel that he can trust to their guidance. His confidence once gained, he may be lured on to the most incredible adventures—as the Arabian Nights are there to show. A wise critic once said: "You may ask your reader to believe anything you can *make* him believe." It is never the *genii* who are unreal, but only their unconvinced historian's description of them. The least touch of irrelevance, the least chill of inattention, will instantly undo the spell, and it will take as long to weave again as to get Humpty Dumpty back on his wall. The moment the reader loses faith in the author's sureness of foot the chasm of improbability gapes.

Improbability in itself, then, is never a danger, but the appearance of improbability is; unless, indeed, the tale be based on what, in my first chapter, I called pathological conditions—conditions of body or mind outside the field of normal experience. But this term, of course, does not apply to states of mind inherited from an earlier phase of race-culture, such as the belief in ghosts. No one with a spark of imagination ever objected to a good ghost story as "improbable"—though Mrs. Barbauld, who doubtless lacked the spark, is said to have condemned "The Ancient Mariner" on this ground. Most of us retain the more or less shadowy memory of ancestral terrors, and airy tongues that syllable men's names. We cannot believe *a priori* in the probability of the actions of madmen, or neurasthenics, because their reasoning processes escape most of us, or can at best be imagined only as belonging to abnormal and exceptional people; but everybody knows a good ghost when he reads about him.

When the reader's confidence is gained the next rule of the game is to avoid distracting and splintering up his attention. Many a would-be tale of horror becomes innocuous through the very multiplication and variety of its horrors. Above all, if they are multiplied they should be cumulative and not dispersed. But the fewer the better: once the preliminary horror posited, it is the harping on the same string—the same nerve—that does the trick. Quiet iteration is far more racking than diversified assaults; the expected is more frightful than the unforeseen. The play of "Emperor Jones" is a striking instance of the power of simplification and repetition to excite in an audience a corresponding state of tension. By sheer voodoo-practice it shows how voodoo acts.

In "The Turn of the Screw"—which stands alone among tales of the supernatural in maintaining the ghostliness of its ghosts not only through a dozen pages but through close on two hundred—the economy of horror is carried to its last degree. What is the reader made to expect? Always—all through the book—that somewhere in that hushed house of doom the poor little governess will come on one of the two figures of evil with whom she is fighting for the souls of her charges. It will be either Peter Quint or the "horror of horrors," Miss Jessel; no diversion from this one dread is ever attempted or expected. It is true that the tale is strongly held together by its profound, its appalling moral significance; but most readers will admit that, long before they are conscious of this, fear, simple shivering animal fear, has them by the throat; which, after all, is what writers of ghost stories are after.

III

It is sometimes said that a "good subject" for a short story should always be capable of being expanded into a novel.

The principle may be defendable in special cases; but it is certainly a misleading one on which to build any general theory. Every "subject" (in the novelist's sense of the term) must necessarily contain within itself its own dimensions; and one of the fiction-writer's essential gifts is that of discerning whether the subject which presents itself to him, asking for incarnation, is suited to the proportions of a short story or of a novel. If it appears to be adapted to both the chances are that it is inadequate to either.

It would be as great a mistake, however, to try to base a hard-and-fast theory on the denial of the rule as on its assertion. Instances of short stories made out of subjects that could have been expanded into a novel, and that are yet typical short stories and not mere stunted novels, will occur to every one. General rules in art are useful chiefly as a lamp in a mine, or a hand-rail down a black stairway; they are necessary for the sake of the guidance they give, but it is a mistake, once they are formulated, to be too much in awe of them.

There are at least two reasons why a subject should find expression in novel-form rather than as a tale; but neither is based on the number of what may be conveniently called incidents, or external happenings, which the narrative contains. There are novels of action which might be condensed into short stories without the loss of their distinguishing qualities. The marks of the subject requiring a longer development are, first, the gradual unfolding of the inner life of its characters, and secondly the need of producing in the reader's mind the sense of the lapse of time. Outward events of the most varied and exciting nature may without loss of probability be crowded into a few hours, but moral dramas usually have their roots deep in the soul, their rise far back in time; and the suddenest-seeming clash in which they culminate should be led up to step by step if it is to explain and justify itself.

There are cases, indeed, when the short story may make use of the moral drama at its culmination. If the incident dealt with be one which a single retrospective flash sufficiently lights up, it is qualified for use as a short story; but if the subject be so complex, and its successive phases so interesting, as to justify elaboration, the lapse of time must necessarily be suggested, and the novel-form becomes appropriate.

The effect of compactness and instantaneity sought in the short story is attained mainly by the observance of two "unities"—the old traditional one of time, and that other, more modern and complex, which requires that any rapidly enacted episode shall be seen through only one pair of eyes.

It is fairly obvious that nothing is more retarding than the marking of a time-interval long enough to suggest modification in the personages of the tale or in their circumstances. The use of such an interval inevitably turns the short story into a long tale unduly compressed, the bald scenario of a novel. In the third chapter, where an attempt will be made to examine the technique of the novel, it will be needful to explore that central mystery—of which Tolstoy was perhaps the one complete master—the art of creating in the reader's mind this sense of passing time. Meanwhile, it may be pointed out that a third, and intermediate, form of tale—the *long* short-story—is available for any subject too spreading for conciseness yet too slight in texture to be stretched into a novel.

The other unity, that of vision, will also be dealt with in considering the novel, in respect of which it becomes a matter much more complicated. Henry James, almost the only novelist who has formulated his ideas about his art, was the first to lay down the principle, though it had long (if intermittently) been observed by the masters of fiction. It may have occurred to other novelists—presumably it has—to ask themselves, as they sat down to write: Who saw this thing I am going to tell about? By whom do I mean that it shall be reported? It seems as though such a question must precede any study of the subject chosen, since the subject is conditioned by the answer; but no critic appears to have propounded it, and it was left to Henry James to do so in one of those entangled prefaces to the Definitive Edition from which the technical axioms ought some day to be piously detached.

It is clear that exactly the same thing never happens to any two people, and that each witness of a given incident will report it differently. Should some celestial taskmaster set the same theme to Jane Austen and George Meredith the bewildered reader would probably have some difficulty in discovering the common denominator. Henry James, in pointing this out, also made the corollary suggestion that the mind chosen by the author to mirror his given case should be so situated, and so constituted, as to take the widest possible view of it.

One thing more is needful for the ultimate effect of probability; and that is, never to let the character who serves as reflector record anything not naturally within his register. It should be the story-teller's first care to choose this reflecting mind deliberately, as one would choose a building-site, or decide upon the orientation of one's house, and when this is done, to live inside the mind chosen, trying to feel, see and react exactly as the latter would, no more, no less, and, above all, no otherwise. Only thus can the writer avoid attributing incongruities of thought and metaphor to his chosen interpreter.

IV

It remains to try to see what constitutes (in any permanent sense) the underlying norm of the "good short story."

A curious distinction between the successful tale and the successful novel at once presents itself. It is safe to say (since the surest way of measuring achievement in art is by survival) that the test of the novel is that its people should be *alive*. No subject in itself, however fruitful, appears to be able to keep a novel alive; only the characters in it can. Of the short story the same cannot be said. Some of the greatest short stories owe their vitality entirely to the dramatic rendering of a situation. Undoubtedly the characters engaged must be a little more than puppets; but apparently, also, they may be a little less than individual human beings. In this respect the short story, rather than the novel, might be called the direct descendant of the old epic or ballad—of those earlier forms of fiction in all of which action was the chief affair, and the characters, if they did not remain mere puppets, seldom or never became more than types—such as the people, for instance, in Molière. The reason of the difference is obvious. Type, general character, may be set forth in a few strokes, but the progression, the unfolding of personality, of which the reader instinctively feels the need if the actors in the tale are to retain their individuality for him through a succession of changing circumstances—this slow but continuous growth requires space, and therefore belongs by definition to a larger, a symphonic plan.

The chief technical difference between the short story and the novel may therefore be summed up by saying that situation is the main concern of the short story, character of the novel; and it follows that the effect produced by the short story depends almost entirely on its form, or presentation. Even more—yes, and much more—than in the construction of the novel, the impression of vividness, of *presentness*, in the affair narrated, has to be sought, and made sure of beforehand, by that careful artifice which is the real carelessness of art. The short-story writer must not only know from what angle to present his anecdote if it is to give out all its fires, but must understand just *why* that particular angle and no other is the right one. He must therefore have turned his subject over and over, walked around it, so to speak, and applied to it those laws of perspective which Paolo Uccello called "so beautiful," before it can be offered to the reader as a natural unembellished fragment of experience, detached like a ripe fruit from the tree.

The moment the writer begins to grope in the tangle of his "material," to hesitate between one and another of the points that any actual happening thrusts up in such disorderly abundance, the reader feels a corresponding hesitancy, and the illusion of reality vanishes. The non-observance of the optics of the printed page results in the same failure to make the subject "carry" as the non-observance of the optics of the stage in presenting a play. By all means let the writer of short stories reduce the technical trick to its minimum—as the cleverest actresses put on the least paint; but let him always bear in mind that the surviving minimum is the only bridge between the reader's imagination and his.

V

Nietzsche said that it took genius to "make an end"— that is, to give the touch of inevitableness to the conclusion of any work of art. In the art of fiction this is peculiarly true of the novel, that slowly built-up monument in which every stone has its particular weight and thrust to carry and of which the foundations must be laid with a view to the proportions of the highest tower. Of the short story, on the contrary, it might be said that the writer's first care should be to know how to make a beginning.

That an inadequate or unreal ending diminishes the short tale in value as much as the novel need hardly be added, since it is proved with depressing regularity by the machine-made "magazine story" to which one or the other of half a dozen "standardized" endings is automatically adjusted at the four-thousand-five-hundredth word of whatsoever has been narrated. Obviously, as every subject contains its own dimensions, so is its conclusion *ab ovo;* and the failure to end a tale in accordance with its own deepest sense must deprive it of meaning.

None the less, the short-story writer's first concern, once he has mastered his subject, is to study what musicians call the "attack." The rule that the first page of a novel ought to contain the germ of the whole is even more applicable to the short story, because in the latter case the trajectory is so short that flash and sound nearly coincide.

Benvenuto Cellini relates in his Autobiography that one day, as a child, while he sat by the hearth with his father, they both saw a salamander in the fire. Even then the sight must have been unusual, for the father instantly boxed his son's ears so that he should never forget what he had seen.

This anecdote might serve as an apothegm for the writer of short stories. If his first stroke be vivid and telling the reader's attention will be instantly won. The " 'Hell,' said the Duchess as she lit her cigar" with which an Eton boy is said to have begun a tale for his school magazine, in days when Duchesses less commonly smoked and swore, would undoubtedly have carried his narrative to posterity if what followed had been at the same level.

This leads to another point: it is useless to box your reader's ear unless you have a salamander to show him. If the heart of your little blaze is not animated by a living, moving *something* no shouting and shaking will fix the anecdote in your reader's memory. The salamander stands for that fundamental significance that made the story worth telling.

The arrest of attention by a vivid opening should be something more than a trick. It should mean that the narrator has so brooded on this subject that it has become his indeed, so made over and synthesized within him that, as a great draughtsman gives the essentials of a face or landscape in a half-a-dozen strokes, the narrator can "situate" his tale in an opening passage which shall be a clue to all the detail eliminated.

The clue given, the writer has only to follow. But his grasp must be firm; he must never for an instant forget what he wants to tell, or why it seemed worth telling. And this intensity of hold on his subject presupposes, before the telling of even a short story, a good deal of thinking over. Just because the limits of the form selected prevent his producing the semblance of reality by elaborating his characters, is the short-story writer the more bound to make real the adventure in itself. A well-known French confectioner in New York was once asked why his chocolate, good as it was, was not equal to that made in Paris. He replied: "Because, on account of the expense, we cannot *work it over* as many times as the French confectioner can." Other homely analogies confirm the lesson: the seemingly simplest sauces are those that have been most cunningly combined and then most completely blent, the simplest-looking dresses those that require most study to design.

The precious instinct of selection is distilled by that long patience which, if it be not genius, must be one of genius's chief reliances in communicating itself. On this point repetition and insistence are excusable: the shorter the story, the more stripped of detail and "cleared for action," the more it depends for its effect not only on the choice of what is kept when the superfluous has been jettisoned, but on the order in which these essentials are set forth.

VI

Nothing but deep familiarity with his subject will protect the short-story writer from another danger: that of contenting himself with a mere sketch of the episode selected. The temptation to do so is all the greater because some critics, in their resentment of the dense and the prolix, have tended to overestimate the tenuous and the tight.

Mérimée's tales are often cited as models of the *conte;* but they are rather the breathless summaries of longer tales than the bold foreshortening of an episode from which all the significance it has to give has been adroitly extracted. It is easy to be brief and sharply outlined if one does away with one or more dimensions; the real achievement, as certain tales of Flaubert's and Turgenev's, of Stevenson's and of Maupassant's show, is to suggest illimitable air within a narrow space.

The stories of the German "romantic," Heinrich von Kleist, have likewise been praised for an extreme economy of material, but they should rather be held up as an awful warning against waste, for in their ingenious dovetailing of improbable incidents, the only economy practised is that of leaving out all that would have enriched the subject, visually or emotionally. One, indeed, "The Marquise d'O." (thrift is carried so far that the characters are known merely by their initials), has in it the making of a good novel, not unlike Goethe's "Elective Affinities"; but reduced to the limits of a short story it offers a mere skeleton of its subject.

The phrase "economy of material" suggests another danger to which the novelist and the writer of short stories are equally exposed. Such economy is, in both cases, nearly always to be advised in the multiplication of accidental happenings, minor episodes, surprises and contrarieties. Most beginners crowd into their work twice as much material of this sort as it needs. The reluctance to look deeply enough into a subject leads to the indolent habit of decorating its surface. I was once asked to read a manuscript on the eternal theme of a lovers' quarrel. The quarrelling pair made up, and the reasons for dispute and reconciliation were clearly inherent in their characters and situation; but the author, being new at the trade, felt obliged to cast about for an additional, a fortuitous, pretext for their reunion——so he sent them for a drive, made the horses run away, and caused the young man to save the young lady's life. This is a crude example of a frequent fault. Again and again the novelist passes by the real meaning of a situation simply for lack of letting it reveal all its potentialities instead of dashing this way and that in quest of fresh effects. If, when once drawn to a subject, he would let it grow slowly in his mind instead of hunting about for arbitrary combinations of circumstance, his tale would have the warm scent and flavour of a fruit ripened in the sun instead of the insipidity of one forced in a hot-house.

There is a sense in which the writing of fiction may be compared to the administering of a fortune. Economy and expenditure must each bear a part in it, but they should never degenerate into parsimony or waste. True economy consists in the drawing out of one's subject of every drop of significance it can give, true expenditure in devoting time, meditation and patient labour to the process of extraction and representation.

It all comes back to a question of expense: expense of time, of patience, of study, of thought, of letting hundreds of stray experiences accumulate and group themselves in the memory, till suddenly one of the number emerges and throws its sharp light on the subject which solicits you. It has been often, and inaccurately, said that the mind of a creative artist is a mirror, and the work of art the reflection of life in it. The mirror, indeed, is the artist's mind, with all his experiences reflected in it; but the work of art, from the smallest to the greatest, should be something projected, not reflected, something on which his mirrored experiences, at the right conjunction of the stars, are to be turned for its full illumination.

III

Constructing a Novel

III

Constructing a Novel

I

For convenience of division it may be said that the novel of psychology was born in France, the novel of manners in England, and that out of their union in the glorious brain of Balzac sprang that strange chameleon-creature, the modern novel, which changes its shape and colour with every subject on which it rests.

In the general muster the novel of manners will be found to have played the most important part; and here English influences preponderate. If innate aptitude were enough for the producing of a work of art, the flowering of the English novel of manners in the late eighteenth and early nineteenth centuries might have surpassed in quality, and intrinsic importance, that of all other schools.

Balzac's debt to Scott has already been touched on; that of the earlier French fiction to Richardson and Sterne is a commonplace in the history of the novel. But the true orientation of English fiction was away from the fine-drawn analysis of Richardson, the desultory humours of Sterne, in the direction of an ample and powerful novel of manners. Smollett and Fielding brought fresh air and noise, the rough-and-tumble of the street, the ribaldry of the tavern, into the ceremonious drawing-rooms depicted by Richardson and later by Miss Burney. The great, the distinguishing gift of the English novelist was a homely simplicity combined with an observation at once keen and indulgent; good-humour was the atmosphere and irony the flavour of this great school of observers, from Fielding to George Eliot.

Till the day of Jane Austen it had been possible to treat without apology of the mixed affair of living; but Jane Austen's delicate genius flourished on the very edge of a tidal wave of prudery. Already Scott was averting his eyes from facts on which the maiden novelist in her rectory parlour had looked unperturbed; when Thackeray and Dickens rose in their might the chains were forged and the statues draped. In the melancholy preface to "Pendennis" Thackeray puts the case bitterly and forcibly: "Since the author of *Tom Jones* was buried, no writer of fiction among us has been permitted to depict to his utmost power a MAN"; and the stunted conclusion of a tale so largely begun testifies to the benumbing effect of the new restrictions. The novels of Charlotte Brontë, which now seem in some respects so romantically unreal, were denounced for sensuality and immorality; and for a time English fiction was in danger of dwindling to the pale parables of Miss Mulock and Miss Yonge.

But for this reaction against truth, this sudden fear of touching on any of the real issues of the human comedy and tragedy, Thackeray's natural endowment would have placed him with the very greatest; Trollope might conceivably have been a lesser Jane Austen; and George Eliot, perhaps born with the richest gifts of any English novelist since Thackeray, might have poured out her treasures of wit and irony and tenderness without continually pausing to denounce and exhort.

But the artist depends on atmosphere for the proper development of his gift; and all these novelists were cramped by the hazard of a social convention from which their continental contemporaries had the good fortune to escape. The artist of other races has always been not only permitted but enjoined to see life whole; and it is this, far more than any superiority of genius, that lifts Balzac, Stendhal and Tolstoy so high above even Thackeray when the universal values are to be appraised. The great continental novelists are all the avowed debtors of their English predecessors; they took the English novel of manners in its amplitude, its merriment and pathos, and in their hands "the thing became a trumpet."

In one respect the English novelists are still supreme; and that is in the diffusion of good humour, good manners one might almost say, which envelops their comedy and tragedy. Much that is savage and acrimonious in the French, dolorous and overwrought in the Russians, is strained away through this fine English *bonhomie,* leaving a clear, bright draught, not very intoxicating or even stimulating, but refreshing and full of a lasting savour. Nor does this prevalent good humour hinder the full expression of tragedy; it helps rather to extract the final bitterness from certain scenes in "Pendennis" and "Vanity Fair," in "Middlemarch" and the "Chronicles of Barsetshire." The last years of Lydgate, the last hour of Mrs. Proudie, seem the more terrible for being muffled in a secure and decent atmosphere of fair play and plumpudding.

Since then all the restraints of prudery which hampered the English novelists of the nineteenth century have come down with a crash, and the "now-that-it-can-be-told-school" (as some one has wittily named it) has rushed to the opposite excess of dirt-for-dirt's sake, from which no real work of art has ever sprung. Such a reaction was inevitable. No one who remembers that Butler's great novel, "The Way of All Flesh," remained unpublished for over twenty years because it dealt soberly but sincerely with the chief springs of human conduct can wonder that laborious monuments of schoolboy pornography are now mistaken for works of genius by a public ignorant of Rabelais and unaware of Apuleius. The balance will right itself with the habit of freedom. The new novelists will learn that it is even more necessary to see life steadily than to recount it whole; and by that time a more thoughtful public may be ripe for the enjoyment of a riper art.

II

Most novels, for convenient survey, may be grouped under one or the other of three types: manners, character (or psychology) and adventure. These designations may be thought to describe the different methods sufficiently; but as a typical example of each, "Vanity Fair" for the first, "Madame Bovary" for the second, and, for the third, "Rob Roy" or "The Master of Ballantrae," might be named.

This grouping must be further stretched to include as subdivisions what might be called the farcical novel of manners, the romance and the philosophical romance; and immediately "Pickwick" for the first, "Harry Richmond," "La Chartreuse de Parme" or "Lorna Doone" for the second, and "Wilhelm Meister" or "Marius the Epicurean" for the third category, suggest themselves to the reader.

Lastly, in the zone of the unclassifiable float such enchanting hybrids as "John Inglesant," "Lavengro," and that great Swiss novel, "Der Grüne Heinrich," in which fantasy, romance and the homeliest realities are so inimitably mingled. It will be noticed that in the last two groups—of romance pure or hybrid—but one French novel has been cited. The French genius, which made "Romanticism" its own (after borrowing it from England), has seldom touched even the hem of Romance: Tristan and Iseult and their long line of descendants come from Broceliande, not from the Ile de France.

Before going farther it should be added that, in a study of the modern novel, the last-named of the three principal groups, the novel of adventure, is the least important because the least modern. That this implies any depreciation of the type in itself will not for a moment be admitted by a writer whose memory rings with the joyous clatter of Dumas the elder, Herman Melville, Captain Marryat and Stevenson; but their gallant yarns might have been sung to the minstrel's harp before Roland and his peers, and told in Babylonian bazaars to Joseph and his Brethren: the tale of adventure is essentially the parent-stock of all subsequent varieties of the novel, and its modern tellers have introduced few innovations in what was already a perfect formula, created in the dawn of time by the world-old appeal: "Tell us another story."

All attempts at classification may seem to belong to school-examinations and textbooks, and to reduce the matter to the level of the famous examination-paper which, in reference to Wordsworth's "O cuckoo, shall I call thee bird, or but a wandering voice?" instructed the student to "state alternative preferred, with reasons for your choice." In a sense, classification is always arbitrary and belittling; yet to the novelist's mind such distinctions represent organic realities. It does not much matter under what heading a school-girl is taught to class "Vanity Fair"; but from the creator's point of view classification means the choice of a manner and of an angle of vision, and it mattered greatly that Thackeray knew just how he meant to envisage his subject, which might have been dealt with merely as the tale of an adventuress, or merely as the romance of an honest couple, or merely as an historical novel, and is all of these, and how much more besides—is, indeed, all that its title promises.

The very fact that so many subjects contain the elements of two or three different types of novel makes it one of the novelist's first cares to decide which method he means to use. Balzac, for instance, gives us in "Le Père Goriot" and in "Eugénie Grandet" two different ways of dealing with subjects that contain, after all, much the same elements; in the one, englobing his tragic father in a vast social panorama, in the other projecting his miser (who should have given the tale its name) in huge Molièresque relief against the narrow background of a sleepy provincial town peopled by three or four carefully-subordinated characters.

There is another kind of hybrid novel, but in which the manner rather than the matter may be so characterized; the novel written almost entirely in dialogue, after the style, say, of "Gyp's" successful tales. It is open to discussion whether any particular class of subjects calls for this treatment. Henry James thought so, and the oddly-contrived "Awkward Age" was a convinced attempt on his part to write "a little thing in the manner of Gyp"—a resemblance which few readers would have perceived had he not pointed it out. Strangely enough, he was persuaded that certain subjects not falling into the stage-categories require nevertheless to be chattered rather than narrated; and, more strangely still, that "The Awkward Age," that delicate and subtle case, all half-lights and shades, all innuendoes, gradations and transitions, was typically made for such treatment.

His hyper-sensitiveness to any comment on his own work made it difficult to discuss the question with him; but his greatest admirers will probably feel that "The Awkward Age" lost more than it gained by being powdered into dialogue, and that, had it been treated as a novel instead of a kind of hybrid play, the obligation of "straight" narrative might have compelled him to face and elucidate the central problem instead of suffering it to lose itself in a tangle of talk. At any rate, such an instance will probably not do much to convince either novelists or their readers of the advantage of the "talked" novel. As a matter of fact, the mode of presentation to the reader, that central difficulty of the whole affair, must always be determined by the nature of the subject; and the subject which instantly calls for dialogue seems as instantly to range itself among those demanding for their full setting-forth the special artifices of the theatre.

The immense superiority of the novel for any subject in which "situation" is not paramount is just that freedom, that ease in passing from one form of presentation to another, and that possibility of explaining and elucidating by the way, which the narrative permits. Convention is the first necessity of all art; but there seems no reason for adding the shackles of another form to those imposed by one's own. Narrative, with all its suppleness and variety, its range from great orchestral effects to the frail vibration of a single string, should furnish the substance of the novel; dialogue, that precious adjunct, should never be more than an adjunct, and one to be used as skillfully and sparingly as the drop of condiment which flavours a whole dish.

The use of dialogue in fiction seems to be one of the few things about which a fairly definite rule may be laid down. It should be reserved for the culminating moments, and regarded as the spray into which the great wave of narrative breaks in curving toward the watcher on the shore. This lifting and scattering of the wave, the coruscation of the spray, even the mere material sight of the page broken into short, uneven paragraphs, all help to reinforce the contrast between such climaxes and the smooth effaced gliding of the narrative intervals; and the contrast enhances that sense of the passage of time for the producing of which the writer has to depend on his intervening narration. Thus the sparing use of dialogue not only serves to emphasize the crises of the tale but to give it as a whole a greater effect of continuous development.

Another argument against the substitution of dialogue for narrative is the wastefulness and round-aboutness of the method. The greater effect of animation, of presentness, produced by its excessive use will not help the reader through more than half the book, whatever its subject; after that he will perceive that he is to be made to pay before the end for his too facile passage through the earlier chapters. The reason is inherent in the method. When, in real life, two or more people are talking together, all that is understood between them is left out of their talk; but when the novelist uses conversation as a means not only of accentuating but of carrying on his tale, his characters have to tell each other many things that each already knows the other knows. To avoid the resulting shock of improbability, their dialogue must be so diluted with irrelevant touches of realistic commonplace, with what might be described as by-talk, that, as in the least good of Trollope's tales, it rambles on for page after page before the reader, resignedly marking time, arrives, bewildered and weary, at a point to which one paragraph of narrative could have carried him.

III

In writing of the short story I may have seemed to dwell too much on the need of considering every detail in its plan and development; yet the short story is an improvisation, the temporary shelter of a flitting fancy, compared to the four-square and deeply-founded monument which the novel ought to be.

It is not only that the scale is different; it is because of the reasons for its being so. If the typical short story be the foreshortening of a dramatic climax connecting two or more lives, the typical novel usually deals with the gradual unfolding of a succession of events divided by intervals of time, and in which many people, in addition to the principal characters, play more or less subordinate parts. No need now to take in sail and clear the decks; the novelist must carry as much canvas and as many passengers as his subject requires and his seamanship permits.

Still, the novel-theme is distinguished from that suited to the short story not so much by the number of characters presented as by the space required to mark the lapse of time or to permit the minute analysis of successive states of feeling. The latter distinction, it should be added, holds good even when the states of feeling are all contained in one bosom, and crowded into a short period, as they are in "The Kreutzer Sonata." No one would think of classing "The Kreutzer Sonata," or "Ivan Ilyitch," or "Adolphe," among short stories; and such instances prove the difficulty of laying down a hard-and-fast distinction between the forms. The final difference lies deeper. A novel may be all about one person, and about no more than a few hours in that person's life, and yet not be reducible to the limits of a short story without losing all significance and interest. It depends on the character of the subject chosen.

Since the novel-about-one-person has been touched on, it may be well, before going farther, to devote a short parenthesis to its autobiographical or "subjective" variety. In the study of novel-technique one might almost set aside the few masterpieces in this class, such as the "Princesse de Clèves," "Adolphe" and "Dominique," as not novels at all, any more than Musset's "Confession d'un Enfant du Siècle" is a novel. They are, in fact, all fragments of autobiography by writers of genius; and the autobio-graphical gift does not seem very closely related to that of fiction. In the case of the authors mentioned, none but Madame de La Fayette ever published another novel, and her other attempts were without interest. In all the arts abundance seems to be one of the surest signs of vocation. It exists on the lowest scale, and, in the art of fiction, belongs as much to the producer of "railway novels" as to Balzac, Thackeray or Tolstoy; yet it almost always marks the great creative artist. Whatever a man has it in him to do really well he usually keeps on doing with an inde-structible persistency.

There is another sign which sets apart the born novel-ist from the authors of self-confessions in novel-form; that is, the absence of the objective faculty in the latter. The subjective writer lacks the power of getting far enough away from his story to view it as a whole and relate it to its setting; his minor characters remain the mere satellites of the principal personage (himself), and disappear when not lit up by their central luminary.

Such books are sometimes masterpieces; but if by the term "art of fiction" be understood the creation of imag-inary characters and the invention of their imaginary experiences—and there seems no more convenient def-inition—then the autobiographical tale is not strictly a novel, since no objectively creative effort has gone to its making.

It does not follow that born novelists never write autobiographical novels. Instances to the contrary will occur to every one and none more obvious than that of "The Kreutzer Sonata." There is a gulf between such a book and "Adolphe." Tolstoy's tale, though almost avowedly the study of his own tortured soul, is as objective as Othello. The magic transposition has taken place; in reading the story we do not feel ourselves to be in a resuscitated *real world* (a sort of Tussaud Museum of wax figures with actual clothes on), but in that other world which is the image of life transposed in the brain of the artist, a world wherein the creative breath has made all things new. If one happened to begin one's acquaintance with Tolstoy by reading "The Kreutzer Sonata" one would not need to be told that it was the creation of a brain working objectively, a brain which had produced, or was likely to produce, other novels of a wholly different kind; whereas of such books as "Dominique" or "Adolphe," were one to light on them as unpreparedly, one would say: "This is not the invention of a novelist but the self-analysis of a man of genius."

There is one famous book which might be described as the link between the real novel and the autobiography in novel-disguise. This is Goethe's "Werther." Here a youth of genius, as yet unpractised in the art of fiction, has related, under the thinnest of concealments, the story of his own unhappy love. The tale is intensely subjective. The hero is never once *seen from the outside,* the minor figures are hardly drawn out of the limbo of the unrealized; yet how instantly the difference between "Werther" and "Adolphe" declares itself! The latter tale is completely self-contained;

it never suggests in the writer the power or the desire to project a race of imaginary characters. "Werther" does. Every page thrills with the dawning gift of creation. The lover has not been too much absorbed in his own anguish to turn its light on things external to him. The young Goethe who has noted Charlotte's way of cutting the bread-and-butter for her little brothers and sisters, and set down the bourgeois humours and the sylvan charm of the ball in the forest, is already a novelist.

IV

The question of form—already defined as the order, in time and importance, in which the incidents of the narrative are grouped—is, for obvious reasons, harder to deal with in the novel than in the short story, and most difficult in the novel of manners, with its more crowded stage, and its continual interweaving of individual with social analysis.

The English novelists of the early nineteenth century were still farther enslaved by the purely artificial necessity of the double plot. Two parallel series of adventures, in which two separate groups of people were concerned, sometimes with hardly a link between the two, and always without any deep organic connection, were served up in alternating sections. Throughout the novels of Dickens, George Eliot, Trollope and the majority of their contemporaries, this tedious and senseless convention persists, checking the progress of each series of events and distracting the reader's attention. The artificial trick of keeping two stories going like a juggler's ball is entirely different from the attempt to follow the interwoven movements of typical social groups, as Thackeray did in "Vanity Fair" and "The Newcomes," Balzac in "Le Père Goriot." In these cases the separate groups, either families or larger units, in a sense impersonate *the protagonists of the tale,* and their fates are as closely interwoven as those of the two or three persons on the narrow stage of a tale like "Silas Marner."

The double plot has long since vanished, and the "plot" itself, in the sense of an elaborate puzzle into which a given number of characters have to be arbitrarily fitted, has gone with it to the lumber-room of discarded conventions. But traces of the parallel story linger in the need often felt by young writers of crowding their scene with supernumeraries. The temptation is specially great in composing the novel of manners. If one is undertaking to depict a "section of life," how avoid a crowded stage? The answer is, by choosing as principal characters figures so typical that each connotes a whole section of the social background. It is the unnecessary characters who do the crowding, who confuse the reader by uselessly dispersing his attention; but even the number of subordinate yet necessary characters may be greatly reduced by making the principal figures so typical that they adumbrate most of the others.

The traditions of the Théâtre Français used to require that the number of objects on the stage—chairs, tables, even to a glass of water on a table—should be limited to the actual requirements of the drama: the chairs must all be sat in, the table carry some object necessary to the action, the glass of water or decanter of wine be a part of the drama.

The stage-realism introduced from England a generation ago submerged these scenic landmarks under a flood of irrelevant upholstery; but as guides in the labyrinth of composition they are still standing, as necessary to the novelist as to the playwright. In both cases a far profounder effect is produced by the penetrating study of a few characters than by the multiplying of half-drawn figures. Neither novelist nor playwright should ever venture on creating a character without first following it out to the end of the projected tale and being sure that the latter will be the poorer for its absence. Characters whose tasks have not been provided for them in advance are likely to present as embarrassing problems as other types of the unemployed.

In the number of characters introduced, as much as in the scenic details given, relevance is the first, the arch, necessity. And characters and scenic detail are in fact one to the novelist who has fully assimilated his material. The moon-enchanted hollow of Wilming Weir in "Sandra Belloni" is as much the landscape of Emilia's soul as of a corner of England; it was one of George Meredith's distinguishing merits that he always made his art as a landscape-painter contribute to the interpretation of his tale, so that such scenes as that of Wilming Weir, the sunrise from the top of Monte Motterone in the opening chapter of "Vittoria," and the delicious wall-flower-coloured picture of the farm-house in "Harry Richmond," are all necessary parts of the novels in which they figure, and above all are seen as the people *to whom they happened* would have seen them.

This leads to another important principle. The impression produced by a landscape, a street or a house should always, to the novelist, be an event in the history of a soul, and the use of the "descriptive passage," and its style, should be determined by the fact that it must depict only what the intelligence concerned would have noticed, and always in terms within the register of that intelligence. Two instances, illustrating respectively the observance and the neglect of this rule, may be cited from the novels of Mr. Hardy: the first, that memorable evocation of Egdon Heath by night, as Eustacia Vye looks forth on it from Rainbarrow; the other, the painfully detailed description, in all its geological and agricultural details, of the Wessex vale through which another of Mr. Hardy's heroines, unseeing, wretched, and incapable at any time of noting such particularities as it has amused her creator to set down, flies blindly to her doom.

V

The two central difficulties of the novel—both of which may at first appear purely technical—are still to be considered. They have to do with the choice of the point from which the subject is to be seen, and with the attempt to produce on the reader the effect of the passage of time.

Both may "appear purely technical"; but even were it possible to draw a definite line between the technique of a work of art and its informing spirit, the points in question go too deep to be so classed. They are rooted in the subject; and—as always, in the last issue—the subject itself must determine and limit their office.

It was remarked in the chapter on the short story that the same experience never happens to any two people, and that the story-teller's first care, after the choice of a subject, is to decide to which of his characters the episode in question happened, since it could not have happened in that particular way to more than one. Applied to the novel this may seem a hard saying, since the longer passage of time and more crowded field of action presuppose, on the part of the visualizing character, a state of omniscience and omnipresence likely to shake the reader's sense of probability. The difficulty is most often met by shifting the point of vision from one character to another, in such a way as to comprehend the whole history and yet preserve the unity of impression. In the interest of this unity it is best to shift as seldom as possible, and to let the tale work itself out from not more than two (or at most three) angles of vision, choosing as reflecting consciousnesses persons either in close mental and moral relation to each other, or discerning enough to estimate each other's parts in the drama, so that the latter, even viewed from different angles, always presents itself to the reader *as a whole*.

The choice of such reflectors is not easy; still more arduous is the task of determining at what point each is to be turned on the scene. The only possible rule seems to be that when things happen which the first reflector cannot, with any show of probability, be aware of, or is incapable of reacting to, even if aware, then another, an adjoining, consciousness is required to take up the tale.

Thus drily stated, the formula may seem pedantic and arbitrary; but it will be found to act of itself in the hands of the novelist who has so let his subject ripen in his mind that the characters are as close to him as his own flesh. To the novelist who lives among his creations in this continuous intimacy they should pour out their tale almost as if to a passive spectator.

The problem of the co-ordinating consciousness has visibly disturbed many novelists, and the different solutions attempted are full of interest and instruction. Each is of course but another convention, and no convention is in itself objectionable, but becomes so only when wrongly used, as dirt, according to the happy definition, is only "matter in the wrong place."

Verisimilitude is the truth of art, and any convention which hinders the illusion is obviously in the wrong place. Few hinder it more than the slovenly habit of some novelists of tumbling in and out of their characters' minds, and then suddenly drawing back to scrutinize them from the outside as the avowed Showman holding his puppets' strings. All the greatest modern novelists have felt this, and sought, though often half-unconsciously, to find a way out of the difficulty. The most interesting experiments made in this respect have

been those of James and Conrad, to both of whom—
though in ways how different!—the novel was always by
definition a work of art, and therefore worthy of the
creator's utmost effort.

James sought the effect of verisimilitude by rigorously
confining every detail of his picture to the range, and also
to the capacity, of the eye fixed on it. "In the Cage" is a
curiously perfect example of the experiment on a small
scale, only one very restricted field of vision being permitted. In his longer and more eventful novels, where the
transition from one consciousness to another became
necessary, he contrived it with such unfailing ingenuity
that the reader's visual range was continuously enlarged by
the substitution of a second consciousness whenever the
boundaries of the first were exceeded. "The Wings of the
Dove" gives an interesting example of these transitions. In
"The Golden Bowl," still unsatisfied, still in pursuit of an
impossible perfection, he felt he must introduce a sort of
co-ordinating consciousness detached from, but including, the
characters principally concerned. The same attempt to
wrest dramatic forms to the uses of the novel that caused
"The Awkward Age" to be written in dialogue seems to
have suggested the creation of Colonel and Mrs.
Assingham as a sort of Greek chorus to the tragedy of
"The Golden Bowl." This insufferable and incredible
couple spend their days in espionage and delation, and
their evenings in exchanging the reports of their eaves'-
dropping with a minuteness and precision worthy of
Scotland Yard. The utter improbability of such conduct on
the part of a dull-witted and frivolous couple in the rush

of London society shows that the author created them for the sole purpose of revealing details which he could not otherwise communicate without lapsing into the character of the mid-Victorian novelist chatting with his readers of "my heroine" in the manner of Thackeray and Dickens. Convention for convention (and both are bad), James's is perhaps even more unsettling to the reader's confidence than the old-fashioned intrusion of the author among his puppets. Both ought to be avoided, and may be, as other great novels are there to prove.

Conrad's preoccupation was the same, but he sought to solve it in another way, by creating what someone has aptly called a "hall of mirrors," a series of reflecting consciousnesses, all belonging to people who are outside of the story but accidentally drawn into its current, and not, like the Assinghams, forced into it for the sole purpose of acting as spies and eaves'-droppers.

The method did not originate with Conrad. In that most perfectly-composed of all short stories, "La Grande Bretèche," Balzac showed what depth, mystery, and verisimilitude may be given to a tale by causing it to be reflected, in fractions, in the minds of a series of accidental participants or mere lookers-on. The relator of the tale, casually detained in a provincial town, is struck by the ruinous appearance of one of its handsomest houses. He makes his way into the deserted garden, and is at once called on by a solicitor who informs him that, according to the will of the lately deceased owner, no one is to be permitted on the premises till fifty years after her death. The visitor, whose curiosity is naturally excited, next learns from the landlady of his inn that, though she has never known the exact facts of the tragedy, she knows there has been one, and that a person whom she suspects of having played a part in it is actually lodged under her roof. From the landlady the narrator carries his enquiries to the maid-servant of the inn, who had been in the service of the dead lady, and who confides to him the dreadful scenes of which she was a helpless and horror-struck witness; and, grouping these fragments in his own more comprehending mind, he finally gives them to the reader in their ghastly completeness.

Even George Meredith, whose floods of improvisation seem to have been so rarely hampered by any concern as to the composition of his novels, was now and then visibly perplexed by the question of how to pass from the mind of one character to another without too violent a jolt to the reader. In one instance—in one of those "big scenes" which, as George Eliot said, "write themselves"—he attempted, probably on the spur of the moment, a solution which proved admirably successful—for that particular occasion. In the memorable talk in the course of which the inarticulate Rhoda Fleming and her tongue-tied suitor finally discover themselves to each other, the novelist, to show how tongue-tied both were, and yet convey the emotion beneath their halting monosyllables, hit on the device of putting in parenthesis, after each phrase, what the speaker was actually thinking. It is one of the great pages of the book; yet even in the enchantment of first reading it one is aware of admiring a mere acrobatic feat, a sort of breathless *chassé-croisé* which could not have been kept up for another page without straining the reader's patience and his sense of likelihood. Meredith was a genius, and his instinct for effect made him, at a crucial moment, stumble on a successful trick; but, because he was a genius, he did not prolong or repeat it.

The reason why such sudden changes from one mind to another are fatiguing and disillusioning was summed up—though for a different purpose—in a vivid phrase of George Eliot's. It is in the chapter of "Middlemarch" which records the talk between Dorothea and Celia Brooke, after the latter's first meeting with the austere and pompous Mr. Casaubon, whom her elder sister so unaccountably admires. The frivolous Celia is profoundly disappointed: she finds Mr. Casaubon very ugly. Dorothea, at this, haughtily lets drop that he reminds her of the portraits of Locke. Celia: "Had Locke those two white moles with hairs on them?" Dorothea: "*Oh, I daresay! when people of a certain sort looked at him.*"

That answer sums up the whole dilemma. Before beginning his tale, the novelist must decide whether it is to be seen through eyes given to noting white moles, or to discovering "the visionary butterfly alit" on faces so disfigured. He cannot have it both ways and still hope to persuade his reader.

The other difficulty is that of communicating the effect of the gradual passage of time in such a way that the modifying and maturing of the characters shall seem not an arbitrary sleight-of-hand but the natural result of growth in age and experience. This is the great mystery of the art of fiction. The secret seems incommunicable; one can only conjecture that it has to do with the novelist's own deep belief in his characters and what he is telling about them. He *knows* that this and that befell them, and that in the interval between this and that the months and years have continued their slow task of erosion or accretion; and he conveys this knowledge by some subterranean process as hard to seize in action as the growth of a plant. A study of the great novelists— and especially of Balzac, Thackeray, and Tolstoy—will show that such changes are suggested, are arrived at, in the inconspicuous transitional pages of narrative that lead from climax to climax. One of the means by which the effect is produced is certainly that of not fearing to go slowly, to keep down the tone of the narrative, to be as colourless and quiet as life often is in the intervals between its high moments.

Another difficulty connected with this one is that of keeping so firm a hold on the main lines of one's characters that they emerge modified and yet themselves from the ripening or disintegrating years. Tolstoy had this gift to a supreme degree. Wherever in the dense forest of "War and Peace" a character reappears, often after an interval so long that the ear has almost lost *the sound to which he rhymes,* he is at once recognized as the same, profoundly the same, yet scored by new lines of suffering and experience. Natacha, grown into the fat slovenly *mère-de-famille* of the last chapters, is incredibly like and yet different to the phantom of delight who first captivated Prince Andrew; and the Prince himself, in those incomparable pages devoted to his long illness, where one watches the very process of dematerialization, the detachment from earthly things happening as naturally as the fall of a leaf, is the same as the restless and unhappy man who appears with his pathetic irritating little wife at the evening party of the first chapter.

Becky Sharp, Arthur Pendennis, Dorothea Casaubon, Lydgate, Charles Bovary—with what sure and patient touches their growth and decline are set forth! And how mysteriously yet unmistakably, as they reappear after each interval, the sense is conveyed that there *has* been an interval, not in moral experience only but in the actual lapse of the seasons! The producing of this impression is indeed the central mystery of the art. To its making go patience, meditation, concentration, all the quiet habits of mind now so little practised, so seldom inculcated; and to these must be added the final imponderable, genius, without which the rest is useless, and which, conversely, would be unusable without the rest.

VI

The evening party with which "War and Peace" begins is one of the most triumphant examples in fiction of the difficult art of "situating" the chief actors in the opening chapter of what is to be an exceptionally crowded novel. No reader is likely to forget, or to confuse the one with

the other, the successive arrivals at that dull and trivial
St. Petersburg reception; Tolstoy with one mighty sweep
gathers up all his principal characters and sets them
before us in action. Very different—though so notable
an achievement in its way—is the first chapter of "The
Karamazoff Brothers" (in the English or German translation—for the current French translation inexplicably
omits it). In this chapter Dostoievsky has hung a gallery
of portraits against a blank wall. He describes all the
members of the Karamazoff family, one after another,
with merciless precision and infernal insight. But there
they remain hanging—or standing. The reader is told all
about them, but is not allowed to surprise them in
action. The story about them begins afterward, whereas
in "War and Peace" the first paragraph leads into the
thick of the tale, and every phrase, every gesture, carries
it on with that slow yet sweeping movement of which
Tolstoy alone was capable.

Many thickly-peopled novels begin more gradually—
like "Vanity Fair," for example—and introduce their
characters in carefully-ordered succession. The process
is obviously simpler, and in certain cases as effective.
The morning stroll of M. and Mme. Reynal and their little boys, in the first chapter of "Le Rouge et le Noir,"
sounds a note sufficiently portentous; and so does Major
Pendennis's solitary breakfast. In a general way there is
much to be said for a quiet opening to a long and
crowded novel; though the novelist might prefer to be
able to fling all his characters on the boards at once, with

Tolstoy's regal prodigality. There is no fixed rule about this, or about any other method; each, in the art of fiction, to justify itself has only to succeed. But to succeed, the method must first of all suit the subject, must find its account, as best it can, with the difficulties peculiar to each situation.

The question *where to begin* is the next to confront the novelist; and the art of seizing on the right moment is even more important than that of being able to present a large number of characters at the outset.

Here again no general rule can be laid down. One subject may require to be treated from the centre, in the fashion dear to Henry James, with its opening in the heart of the action, and retrospective vistas radiating away from it on all sides, while others—of which "Henry Esmond" is one of the most beautiful examples—would lose all their bloom were they not allowed to ripen almost imperceptibly under the reader's absorbed contemplation. Balzac, in his preface to "La Chartreuse de Parme"—almost the only public recognition of Stendhal's genius during the latter's life-time—reproves the author for beginning the book before its real beginning. Balzac knew well enough what the world would have lost had that opening picture of Waterloo been left out; but he insists that it is no part of the story Stendhal had set out to tell, and sums up with the illuminating phrase: "M. Beyle has chosen a subject [the Waterloo episode] *which is real in nature but not in art.*" That is, being out of place in that particular work of art, it loses its reality *as art* and remains merely a masterly study of a corner of a battle-field, the greatest the world was to know till Tolstoy's, but no part of a composition, as Tolstoy's always were.

VII

The length of a novel, more surely even than any of its other qualities, needs to be determined by the subject. The novelist should not concern himself beforehand with the abstract question of length, should not decide in advance whether he is going to write a long or a short novel; but in the act of composition he must never cease to bear in mind that one should always be able to say of a novel: "It might have been longer," never: "It need not have been so long."

Length, naturally, is not so much a matter of pages as of the mass and quality of what they contain. It is obvious that a mediocre book is always too long, and that a great one usually seems too short. But beyond this question of quality and weightiness lies the more closely relevant one of the development which this or that subject requires, the amount of sail it will carry. The great novelists have always felt this, and, within an inch or two, have cut their cloth accordingly.

Mr. A. C. Bradley, in his book on Shakespeare's tragedies, threw a new and striking light on the question of length. In analyzing "Macbeth," which is so much shorter than Shakespeare's other tragedies that previous commentators had always assumed the text to be incomplete, he puts the following questions: If the text is incomplete, at what points are the supposed lacunæ to be found? Does any one, on first reading "Macbeth," feel it to be too short, or even notice that it is appreciably less long than the other tragedies? And if not, is it not probable that we have virtually the whole play before us, and that Shakespeare knew he had made it as long as the subject warranted and the nerves of his audience could stand? Whether or not the argument be thought convincing in the given case, it is an admirable example of the spirit in which works of art should be judged, and of the only system of weights and measures applicable to them.

Tolstoy gave to "Ivan Ilyitch" just enough development to make a parable of universal application out of the story of an insignificant man's death. A little more, and he would have dropped into the fussy and meticulous, and smothered his meaning under unnecessary detail. Maupassant was another writer who had an unerring sense for the amount of sail his subjects could carry; and his work contains no better proof of it than the tale of "Yvette"—that harrowing little record of one of the ways in which the bloom may be brushed from a butterfly.

Henry James, in "The Turn of the Screw," showed the same perfect sense of proportion. He had ventured to expand into a short novel the kind of tale usually imposed on the imagination in a single flash of horror; but his instinct told him that to go farther was impossible. The posthumous fragment, "The Sense of the Past," shows that he was again experimenting with the supernatural as a subject for a long novel; and in this instance one feels that he was about to risk over-burdening his theme. When I read M. Maeterlinck's book on the bee (which had just made a flight into fame as high as that of the insect it celebrates) I was first dazzled, then oppressed, by the number and the choice of his adjectives and analogies. Every touch was effective, every comparison striking; but when I had assimilated them all, and remade out of them the ideal BEE, that animal had become a winged elephant. The lesson was salutary for a novelist.

The great writers of fiction—Balzac, Tolstoy, Thackeray, George Eliot (how one has to return to them!)—all had a sense for the proportion of their subjects, and knew that the great argument requires space. There are few things more exquisite in minor English verse than Ben Jonson's epitaph on Salathiel Pavy; but "Paradise Lost" needs more room, and the fact that it does is one of the elements of its greatness. The point is to know at the start if one has in hand a Salathiel Pavy theme or a "Paradise Lost" one.

In no novelist was this instinct more unerring than in the impeccable Jane Austen. Never is there any danger of finding any of her characters out of proportion or rattling around in their setting. The same may be said of Tolstoy, at the opposite end of the scale. His epic gift—the power of immediately establishing the right proportion between his characters and the scope of their adventure—seems never to have failed him. "War and Peace" and Flaubert's "Education Sentimentale" are two of the longest of modern novels. Flaubert too was endowed with the rare instinct of scale; but there are moments when even his most ardent admirers feel that "L'Education Sentimentale" is too long for its carrying-power: whereas in the very first pages of "War and Peace" Tolstoy manages to establish the right relation between subject and length. But there is another difference between the great novel and the merely long one. Even the longest and most seemingly desultory novels of such writers as Balzac, Flaubert and Tolstoy follow a prescribed orbit; they are true to the eternal effort of art to complete what in life seems incoherent and fragmentary. This sense of the great theme sweeping around on its allotted track in the "most ancient heavens" is communicated on the first page of such novels as "War and Peace" and "L'Education Sentimentale"; it is the lack of this intrinsic form that marks the other kind of long novel as merely long.

M. Romain Rolland's "Jean-Christophe" might be cited as a case in point. In a succession of volumes, planned at the outset as parts of a great whole, he tells a series of consecutive soul-adventures, none without interest; but such hint of scale as there is in the first volume seems to warrant no more than that one, and the reader feels that if there are more there is no reason why there should not be any number. This impression is produced not by the lack of a plan, but of that subtler kind of composition which, inspired by the sense of form, and deducing the length of a book from the importance of its argument, creates figures proportioned to their setting, and launches them with a sure hand on their destined path.

The question of the length of a novel naturally leads to the considering of its end; but of this there is little to be said that has not already been implied by the way, since no conclusion can be right which is not latent in the first page. About no part of a novel should there be a clearer sense of inevitability than about its end; any hesitation, any failure to gather up all the threads, shows that the author has not let his subject mature in his mind. A novelist who does not know when his story is finished, but goes on stringing episode to episode after it is over, not only weakens the effect of the conclusion, but robs of significance all that has gone before.

But if the *form* of the end is inevitably determined by the subject, its style—using the term, in the sense already defined, to describe the way in which the episodes of the narrative "are grasped and coloured by the author's mind"—necessarily depends on his sense of selection. At every stage in the progress of his tale the novelist must rely on what may be called the *illuminating incident* to reveal and emphasize the inner meaning of each situation. Illuminating incidents are the magic casements of fiction, its vistas on infinity. They are also the most personal element in any narrative, the author's most direct contribution; and nothing gives such immediate proof of the quality of his imagination—and therefore of the richness of his temperament—as his choice of such episodes.

Lucien de Rubempé (in "Les Illusions Perdues") writing drinking songs to pay for the funeral of his mistress,

who lies dying in the next room; Henry Esmond watching Beatrix come down the stairs in her scarlet stockings
with silver clocks; Stephen Guest suddenly dazzled by
the curve of Maggie Tulliver's arm as she lifts it to pick a
flower for him in the conservatory; Arabella flinging the
offal across the hedge at Jude; Emma losing her temper
with Miss Bates at the picnic; the midnight arrival of
Harry Richmond's father, in the first chapter of that glorious tale: all these scenes shed a circle of light far
beyond the incident recorded.

At the conclusion of a novel the illuminating incident
need only send its ray backward; but it should send a
long enough shaft to meet the light cast forward from
the first page, as in that poignant passage at the end of
"L'Education Sentimentale" where Mme. Arnoux comes
back to see Frédéric Moreau after long years of separation.

"He put her endless questions about herself and her
husband. She told him that, in order to economize and
pay their debts, they had settled down in a lost corner of
Brittany. Arnoux, almost always ailing, seemed like an
old man. Their daughter was married, at Bordeaux; their
son was in the colonial army, at Mostaganem. She lifted
her head: 'But at last I see you again! I'm happy' . . ." She
asks him to take her for a walk, and wanders with him
through the Paris streets. She is the only woman he has
ever loved, and he knows it now. The intervening years
have vanished, and they walk on, "absorbed in each
other, hearing nothing, as if they were walking in the

country on a bed of dead leaves." Then they return to the young man's rooms, and Mme. Arnoux, sitting down, takes off her hat.

"The lamp, placed on a console, lit up her white hair. *The sight was like a blow on his chest.*" He tries to keep up a pretense of sentimentalizing; but "she watched the clock, and he continued to walk up and down, smoking. Neither could find anything to say to the other. In all separations there comes a moment when the beloved is no longer with us." This is all; but every page that has gone before is lit up by the tragic gleam of Mme. Arnoux's white hair.

The same note is sounded in the chapter of "The Golden Bowl" where the deeply, the doubly betrayed Maggie, walking up and down in the summer evening on the terrace of Fawns, looks in at the window of the smoking-room, where her father, her husband and her step-mother (who is her husband's mistress) are playing bridge together, unconscious of her scrutiny. As she looks she knows that she has them at her mercy, and that they all (even her father) know it; and in the same instant the sight of them tells her that "to feel about them in any of the immediate, inevitable, assuaging ways, the ways usually open to innocence outraged and generosity betrayed, would have been to give them up, *and that giving them up was, marvelously, not to be thought of.*"

The illuminating incident is not only the proof of the novelist's imaginative sensibility; it is also the best means of giving presentness, immediacy, to his tale. Far more than on dialogue does the effect of immediacy depend on the apt use of the illuminating incident; and the more threads of significance are gathered up into each one, the more pages of explanatory narrative are spared to writer and reader. There is a matchless instance of this in "Le Rouge et le Noir." The young Julien Sorel, the tutor of the Reynal children, believes a love-affair with their mother to be the best way of advancing his ambitions, and decides to test his audacity by taking Mme. Reynal's hand as they sit in the garden in the summer dusk. He has a long struggle with his natural timidity and her commanding grace before he can make even this shy advance; and that struggle tells, in half a page, more of his fatuities and meannesses, and the boyish simplicity still underlying them—and more too of the poor proud woman at his side—than a whole chapter of analysis and retrospection. This power to seize his characters in their habit as they live is always the surest proof of a novelist's mastery.

But the choice of the illuminating incident, though so much, is not all. As the French say, *there is the manner*. In Stendhal's plain and straightforward report of the scene in the garden every word, every stroke, tells. And this question of manner—of the particular manner adapted to each scene—brings one to another point at which the novelist's vigilance must never flag. As every tale contains its own dimension, so it implies its own manner, the particular shade of style most fitted to convey its full meaning.

Most novelists who have a certain number of volumes to their credit, and have sought, as the subject required, to vary their manner, have been taken to task alike by readers and reviewers, and either accused of attempting to pass off earlier works on a confiding public, or pitied for a too-evident decline in power. Any change disturbs the intellectual indolence of the average reader; and nothing, for instance, has done more to deprive Stevenson of his proper rank among English novelists than his deplorable habit of not conceiving a boy's tale in the same spirit as a romantic novel or a burlesque detective story, of not even confining himself to fiction, but attempting travels, criticism and verse, and doing them all so well that there must obviously be something wrong about it. The very critics who extol the versatility of the artists of the Renaissance rebuke the same quality in their own contemporaries; and their eagerness to stake out each novelist's territory, and to confine him to it for life, recalls the story of the verger in an English cathedral, who, finding a stranger kneeling in the sacred edifice between services, tapped him on the shoulder with the indulgent admonition: "Sorry, sir, but we can't have any praying here at this hour."

This habit of the reader of wanting each author to give only what he has given before exercises the same subtly suggestive influence as all other popular demands. It is one of the most insidious temptations to the young artist to go on doing what he already knows how to do, and knows he will be praised for doing. But the mere fact that so many people want him to write in a certain way ought to fill him

with distrust of that way. It would be a good thing for letters if the perilous appeal of popularity were oftener met
in the spirit of the New England shop-keeper who, finding
a certain penknife in great demand, did not stock that kind
the following year because, as he said, too many people
came bothering him about it.

VIII

Goethe declared that only the Tree of Life was green,
and that all theories were gray; and he also congratu-
lated himself on never "having thought about thinking."
But if he never thought about thinking he did think a
great deal about his art, and some of the axioms he laid
down for its practice go deeper than those of the pro-
fessed philosophers.

The art of fiction, as now practised, is a recent one, and
the arts in their earliest stages are seldom theorized on by
those engaged in creating them; but as soon as they begin
to take shape their practitioners, or at least those of the
number who happen to think as well as to create, perforce
begin to ask themselves questions. Some may not have
Goethe's gift for formulating the answers, even to themselves; but these answers will eventually be discoverable in
an added firmness of construction and appropriateness of
expression. Other writers do consciously lay down rules,
and in the search for new forms and more complex effects
may even become the slaves of their too-fascinating theories. These are the true pioneers, who are never destined

to see their own work fulfilled, but build intellectual houses for the next generation to live in.

Henry James was of this small minority. As he became more and more preoccupied with the architecture of the novel he unconsciously subordinated all else to his ever-fresh complexities of design, so that his last books are magnificent projects for future masterpieces rather than living creations. Such an admission may seem to reinforce the argument against theorizing about one's art; but there are few Jameses and fewer Goethes in any generation, nor is there ever much danger in urging mankind to follow a counsel of perfection. In the case of most novelists, such thought as they spare to the art, its range and limitations, far from sterilizing their talent will stimulate it by giving them a surer command of their means, and will perhaps temper their eagerness for popular recognition by showing them that the only reward worth having is in the quality of the work done.

The foregoing considerations on the writing of fiction may seem to some dry and dogmatic, to others needlessly complicated; still others may feel that in the quest for an intelligible working theory the gist of the matter has been missed. No doubt there is some truth in all these objections; there would be, even had the subject been far more fully and adequately treated. It would appear that in the course of such enquiries the gist of the matter always does escape. Just as one thinks to cast a net over it, a clap of the wings, and it is laughing down on one from the topmost bough of the Tree of Life!

Is all seeking vain, then? Is it useless to try for a clear view of the meaning and method of one's art? Surely not. If no art can be quite pent-up in the rules deduced from it, neither can it fully realize itself unless those who practise it attempt to take its measure and reason out its processes. It is true that the gist of the matter always escapes, since it nests, the elusive bright-winged thing, in that mysterious fourth-dimensional world which is the artist's inmost sanctuary and on the threshold of which enquiry per-force must halt; but though that world is inaccessible, the creations emanating from it reveal something of its laws and processes.

Here another parenthesis must be opened to point out once more that, though this world the artist builds about him in the act of creation reaches us and moves us through its resemblance to the life we know, yet in the artist's consciousness its essence, the core of it, is other. All worthless fiction and inefficient reviewing are based on the forgetting of this fact. To the artist his world is as solidly real as the world of experience, or even more so, but in a way entirely different; it is a world to and from which he passes without any sense of effort, but always *with an uninterrupted awareness of the passing.* In this world are begotten and born the creatures of his imagination, more living to him than his own flesh-and-blood, but whom he never thinks of as living, in the reader's simpli-fying sense. Unless he keeps his hold on this dual charac-ter of their being, visionary to him, and to the reader real, he will be the slave of his characters and not their master. When I say their master, I do not mean that they are his marionettes and dangle from his strings. Once projected by his fancy they are living beings who live their own lives; but their world is the one consciously imposed on them by their creator. Only by means of this objectivity of the artist can his characters live in art. I have never been much moved by the story of the tears Dickens is supposed to have shed over the death of Little Nell; that is, if they were real material tears, and not distilled from the milk of Paradise. The business of the artist is to make weep, and not to weep, to make laugh, and not to laugh; and unless tears and laughter, and flesh-and-blood, are transmuted by him into the substance that art works in, they are nothing to his purpose, or to ours.

Yet to say this, though it seems the last word, is not all. The novelist to whom this magic world is not open has not even touched the borders of the art, and to its familiars the power of expression may seem innate. But it is not so. The creatures of that fourth-dimensional world are born as helpless as the human animal; and each time the artist passes from dream to execution he will need to find the rules and formulas on the threshold.

IV

Character and Situation in the Novel

IV

Character and Situation in the Novel

I

Definitions, however difficult and inadequate, are the necessary "tools of criticism." To begin, therefore, one may distinguish the novel of situation from that of character and manners by saying that, in the first, the persons imagined by the author almost always spring out of a vision of the situation, and are inevitably conditioned by it, whatever the genius of their creator; whereas in the larger freer form, that of character and manners (or either of the two), the author's characters are first born, and then mysteriously proceed to work out their own destinies. Let it, at any rate, be understood that this rough distinction shall serve in the following pages to mark the difference between the two ways of presenting the subject since most subjects lend themselves to being treated from either point of view.

It is not easy to find, among great novels written in English, examples of novels of pure situation, that is, in which the situation is what the book is remembered by. Perhaps "The Scarlet Letter" might be cited as one of the few obvious examples. In "Tess of the d'Urbervilles," which one is tempted to name also, the study of character is so interwoven with the drama as to raise the story—for all its obvious shortcomings—to the level of those supreme novels which escape classification. For if one remembers Tess's tragedy, still more vividly does one remember Tess herself.

In continental literature several famous books at once present themselves in the situation group. One of the earliest, as it is the most famous, is Goethe's "Elective Affinities," where a great and terrible drama involves characters of which the creator has not managed quite to sever the marionette wires. Who indeed remembers those vague initialled creatures, whom the author himself forgot to pull out of their limbo in his eagerness to mature and polish their ingenious misfortunes?

Tolstoy's "The Kreutzer Sonata" is another book which lives only by force of situation, sustained, of course, by the profound analysis of a universal passion. No one remembers who the people in "The Kreutzer Sonata" were, or what they looked like, or what sort of a house they lived in—but the very roots of human jealousy are laid bare in the picture of the vague undifferentiated husband, a puppet who comes to life only in function of his one ferocious passion. Balzac alone, perhaps, managed to make of his novels of situation—such as "César Birotteau" or "Le Curé de Tours"—such relentless and penetrating character studies that their protagonists and the difficulties which beset them leap together to the memory whenever the tales are named. But this fusion of categories is the prerogative of the few, of those who know how to write all kinds of novels, and who choose, each time, the way best suited to the subject in hand.

Novels preeminently of character, and in which situation, dramatically viewed, is reduced to the minimum, are far easier to find. Jane Austen has given the norm, the ideal, of this type. Of her tales it might almost be said that the reader sometimes forgets what happens to her characters in his haunting remembrance of their foibles and oddities, their little daily round of preoccupations and pleasures. They are "speaking" portraits, following one with their eyes in that uncannily lifelike way that good portraits have, rather than passionate disordered people dragging one impetuously into the tangle of their tragedy, as one is dragged by the characters of Stendhal, Thackeray and Balzac. Not that Jane Austen's characters do not follow their predestined orbit. They evolve as real people do, but so softly, noiselessly, that to follow the development of their history is as quiet a business as watching the passage of the seasons. A sense of her limitations as certain as her sense of her power must have kept her—unconsciously or not—from trying to thrust these little people into great actions, and made her choose the quiet setting which enabled her to round out her portraits as imperceptibly as the sun models a fruit. "Emma" is perhaps the most perfect example in English fiction of a novel in which character shapes events quietly but irresistibly, as a stream nibbles away its banks.

Next to "Emma" one might place, in this category, the masterpiece of a very different hand: "The Egoist" of Meredith. In this book, though by means so alien to Miss Austen's delicate procedure that one balks at the comparison, the fantastic novelist, whose antics too often make one forget his insight, discarding most of his fatiguing follies, gives a rich and deliberate study of a real human being. But he does not quite achieve Jane Austen's success. His Willoughby Patterne is typical before he is individual, while every character in "Emma" is both, and in degrees always perfectly proportioned. Still, the two books are preeminent achievements in the field of pure character-drawing, and one must turn to the greatest continental novelists—to Balzac again (as always), to Stendhal, Flaubert, Dostoievsky, Turgenev, Marcel Proust, and perhaps to the very occasional best of Trollope—to match such searching and elaborate studies.

But among the continental novelists—with few exceptions—the delineation of character is inextricably combined with the study of manners, as for instance in the novels of Tolstoy, of Balzac and of Flaubert. Turgenev, in "Dmitri Rudin," gave the somewhat rare example of a novel made almost entirely out of the portrayal of a single character; as, at the opposite extreme, Samuel Butler's "Way of all Flesh," for all its brilliant character-drawing, is essentially the portrait of a family and a social group—one of the most distinctive novels of "manners" it is possible to find.

Such preliminary suggestions, cursory as they are, may help, better than mere definitions, to keep in mind the differing types of novel in which either character or situation weighs down the scales.

II

The novel, in the hands of English-speaking writers, has always tended, as it rose in value, to turn to pictures of character and manners, however much blent with dramatic episodes, or entangled in what used to be vaguely known as a plot. The plot, in the traditional sense of the term, consisted in some clash of events, or, less often, of character. But it was an arbitrarily imposed and rather spaciously built framework, inside of which the people concerned had room to develop their idiosyncrasies and be themselves, except in the crucial moments when they became the puppets of the plot.

The real novel of situation, a compacter and above all a more inevitable affair, did not, at least on English soil, take shape till "plot," in the old-fashioned sense of a coil of outward happenings, was giving way to the discovery that real drama is soul-drama. The novel of situation, indeed, has never really acclimatized itself in English-speaking countries; whereas in France it seems to have grown naturally from the psychological novel of the seventeenth and eighteenth centuries, wherein the conflict of characters tended from the first to simplify the drawing of *character* and to turn the protagonists into embodiments of a particular passion rather than of a particular person.

From this danger the English novelist has usually been guarded by an inexhaustible interest in personality, and a fancy for loitering by the way. The plots of Scott, Thackeray, Dickens, George Eliot and their successors are almost detachable at will, so arbitrarily are they imposed on the novel of character which was slowly but steadily developing within their lax support, and which became, as the nineteenth century advanced, the typical form of English fiction.

The novel of situation is a different matter. The situation, instead of being imposed from the outside, is the kernel of the tale and its only reason for being. It seizes the characters in its steely grip, and jiu-jitsus them into the required attitude with a relentlessness against which only genius can prevail. In every form of novel it is noticeable that the central characters tend to be the least real. This seems to be partly explained by the fact that these characters, survivors of the old "hero" and "heroine," whose business it was not to be real but to be sublime, are still, though often without the author's being aware of it, the standard-bearers of his convictions or the expression of his secret inclinations. They are *his* in

CHARACTER AND SITUATION IN THE NOVEL

the sense of tending to do and say what he would do, or imagines he would do, in given circumstances, and being mere projections of his own personality they lack the substance and relief of the minor characters, whom he views coolly and objectively, in all their human weakness and inconsequence. But there remains another reason, less often recognized, for the unreality of novel "heroes" and "heroines," a reason especially applicable to the leading figures in the novel of situation. It is that *the story is about them,* and forces them into the shape which its events impose, while the subordinate characters, moving at ease in the interstices of the tale, and free to go about their business in the illogical human fashion, remain real to writer and readers.

This fact, exemplified in all novels, becomes most vivid in the novel of situation, where the characters tend to turn into Laocoöns, and die in the merciless coils of their adventure. This is the extreme point of the difference between the novel of situation and of character, and the cause of the common habit of regarding them as alternative methods of fiction.

III

The thoughtful critic who would be rid of the cheap formulas of fiction-reviewing, and reach some clearer and deeper expression of the sense and limitations of the art, is sure to resent the glib definition of the novel of situation and the novel of character (or manners) as necessarily

95

antithetical and mutually exclusive. The thoughtful critic will be right; and the thoughtful novelist will share his view. What sense is there in such arbitrary divisions, such opposings of one manner to another, when almost all the greatest novels are there, in their versatility and their abundance, to show the glorious possibility of welding both types of fiction into a single masterpiece?

In what category, for instance, should "Anna Karenina" be placed? Undoubtedly in that of novels of character and manners. Yet if one sums up the tale in its rapidity and its vehemence, what situation did Dumas Fils ever devise for his theatre "of situation" half so poignant or so dramatic as that which Tolstoy manages to keep conspicuously afloat on the wide tossing expanse of the Russian social scene? In "Vanity Fair," again, so preeminently a novel of manners, a novel of character, with what dramatic intensity the situation between Becky, Rawdon and Lord Steyne stands out from the rich populous pages, and gathers up into itself all their diffused significance!

The answer is evident: above a certain height of creative capacity the different methods, the seemingly conflicting points of view, are merged in the artist's comprehensive vision, and the situations inherent in his subject detach themselves in strong relief from the fullest background without disturbing the general composition.

But though this is true, it is true only of the greatest novelists—those who, as Matthew Arnold said of Shakespeare, do not abide our question but are free. In them, vast vision is united to equivalent powers of coordination; but more often the novelist who has the creative vision lacks the capacity for co-ordinating and rendering his subject, or at least is unable, in the same creation, to give an equal part to the development of character and to the clash of situation. Owing to the lack of that supreme equipment which always rises above classification most of the novelists have tended to let their work fall into one of the two categories of situation or character, thus fortifying the theory of the superficial critics that life in fiction must be presented either as conflict or as character.

The so-called novel of character, even in less than the most powerful hands, does not, of course, preclude situation in the sense of a dramatic clash. But the novelist develops his tale through a succession of episodes, all in some way illustrative of the manners or the characters out of which the situation is eventually to spring; he lingers on the way, is not afraid of by-paths, and enriches his scene with subordinate pictures, as the mediæval miniaturist encloses his chief subjects in a border of beautiful ornament and delicate vignettes; whereas the novel of situation is, by definition, one in which the problem to be worked out in a particular human conscience, or the clash between conflicting wills, is the novelist's chief if not his only theme, and everything not directly illuminative of it must be left out as irrelevant. This does not mean that in the latter type of tale—as, for instance, in "Tess of the d'Urbervilles"—the episode, the touch of colour or character, is forbidden. The modern novelist of situation does not seem likely to return to the monochrome starkness of "Adolphe" or "La Princesse de Clèves." He uses every scrap of colour, every picturesque by-product of his subject which that subject yields; but he avoids adding to it a single touch, however decoratively tempting, which is not part of the design.

If the two methods are thus contrasted, the novel of character and manners may seem superior in richness, variety and play of light and shade. This does not prove that it is necessarily capable of a greater total effect than the other; yet so far the greatest novels have undoubtedly dealt with character and manners rather than with mere situation. The inference is indeed almost irresistible that the farther the novel is removed in treatment from theatrical modes of expression, the more nearly it attains its purpose as a freer art, appealing to those more subtle imaginative requirements which the stage can never completely satisfy.

When the novelist has been possessed by a situation, and sees his characters hurrying to its culmination, he must have unusual keenness of vision and sureness of hand to fix their lineaments and detain them on their way long enough for the reader to recognize them as real human beings. In the novel of pure situation it is doubtful if this has ever been done with more art than in "The Wrong Box," where Stevenson launched on his roaring torrent of farce a group of *real people,* alive and individual, who keep their reality and individuality till the end. The tears of laughter that the book provokes generally blind the reader to its subtle character-drawing; but, save for the people in "Gil Blas," and the memorable figures of Chicot and Gorenflot in the Dumas cycle headed by "La Dame de Monsoreau," it would be hard, in any tale of action, to find characters as vivid and individual as those which rollick through this glorious farce.

The tendency of the situation to take hold of the novelist's imagination, and to impose its own *tempo* on his tale, can be resisted only by richness and solidity of temperament. The writer must have a range wide enough to include, within the march of unalterable law, all the inconsequences of human desire, ambition, cruelty, weakness and sublimity. He must, above all, bear in mind at each step that his business is not to ask what the situation would be likely to make of his characters, but what his characters, being what they are, would make of the situation. This question, which is the tuning-fork of truth, never needs to be more insistently applied than in writing the dialogue which usually marks the culminating scenes in fiction. The moment the novelist finds that his characters are talking not as they naturally would, but as the situation requires, are visibly lending him a helping hand in the more rapid elucidation of his drama, the moment he hears them saying anything which the stress of their predicament would not naturally bring to their lips, his effect has been produced at the expense of reality, and he will find them turning to sawdust on his hands.

Some novelists, conscious of the danger, and not sufficiently skilled to meet it, have tried to turn it by interlarding these crucial dialogues with irrelevant small-talk, in the hope of thus producing a greater air of reality. But this is to fall again into the trap of what Balzac called "a reality in nature which is not one in art." The object of dialogue is to gather up the loose strands of passion and emotion running through the tale; and the attempt to entangle these threads in desultory chatter about the weather or the village pump proves only that the narrator has not known how to do the necessary work of selection. All the novelist's art is brought into play by such tests. His characters must talk as they would in reality, and yet everything not relevant to his tale must be eliminated. The secret of success lies in his instinct of selection.

These difficulties are not a reason for condemning the novel of situation as an inferior or at least as a not-worth-while form of the art. Inferior to the larger form, the novel of character and manners, it probably is, if only in the matter of scale; but certainly also worth-while, since it is the natural vehicle of certain creative minds. As long as there are novelists whose inventive faculty presents them first with the form, and only after-ward with the substance, of the tales they want to tell, the novel of situation will fill a purpose. But it is pre-cisely this type of mind which needs to be warned against the dangers of the form. When the problem comes to the novelist before he sees the characters engaged in it, he must be all the more deliberate in deal-ing with it, must let it lie in his mind till it brings forth of itself the kind of people who would naturally be involved in that particular plight. The novelist's perma-nent problem is that of making his people at once typical and individual, universal and particular, and in adopting the form of the novel of situation he perpetually runs the risk of upsetting that nice balance of attributes unless he persists in thinking of his human beings first, and of their predicament only as the outcome of what they are.

IV

The predicament—the situation—must still be borne in mind if the novelist approaches his task in another way, and sees his tale as situation illustrating character instead of the reverse.

Even the novel of character and manners can never be without situation, that is, without some sort of climax caused by the contending forces engaged. The conflict, the shock of forces, is latent in every attempt to detach a fragment of human experience and transpose it in terms of art, that is, of completion.

The seeming alternative is to fall back on the "stream of consciousness"—which is simply the "slice-of-life" of the 'eighties renamed—but that method, as has already been pointed out, contains its own condemnation, since every attempt to employ it of necessity involves selection, and selection in the long run must eventually lead to the transposition, the "stylization," of the subject.

Let it be assumed, then, that a predicament there must be, whether worked out in one soul, or created by the shock of opposing purposes. The larger the canvas of the novel—supposing the novelist's powers to be in

scale with his theme—the larger will be the scale of the
predicament. In the great novel of manners in which
Balzac, Thackeray and Tolstoy were preeminent, the conflict engages not only individuals but social groups, and
the individual plight is usually the product—one of the
many products—of the social conflict. There is a sense
in which situation is the core of every tale, and as truly
present in the quiet pages of "Eugénie Grandet" or "Le
Lys dans la Vallée" as in the tense tragedy of "The Return
of the Native," the epic clash of "War and Peace" or the
dense social turmoil of "Vanity Fair."

But the main advantage of the novelist to whom his
subject first presents itself in terms of character, either
individual or social, is that he can quietly watch his people
or his group going about their business, and let the form
of his tale grow out of what they are, out of their idiosyncrasies, their humours and their prejudices, instead
of fitting a situation onto them before he really knows
them, either personally or collectively.

It is manifest that every method of fiction has its dangers, and that the study of character pursued to excess
may tend to submerge the action necessary to illustrate
that character. In the inevitable reaction against the arbitrary "plot" many novelists have gone too far in the other
direction, either swamping themselves in the tedious
"stream of consciousness," or else—another frequent
error—giving an exaggerated importance to trivial incidents when the tale is concerned with trivial lives. There
is a sense in which nothing which receives the touch

of art is trivial; but to rise to this height the incident, insignificant in itself, must illustrate some general law, and turn on some deep movement of the soul. If the novelist wants to hang his drama on a button, let it at least be one of Lear's.

All things hold together in the practice of any art, and character and manners, and the climaxes springing out of them, cannot, in the art of fiction, be dealt with separately without diminution to the subject. It is a matter for the novelist's genius to combine all these ingredients in their due proportion; and then we shall have "Emma" or "The Egoist" if character is to be given the first place, "Le Père Goriot" or "Madame Bovary" if drama is to be blent with it, and "War and Peace," "Vanity Fair," "L'Education Sentimentale" if all the points of view and all the methods are to be harmonized in the achievement of a great picture wherein the individual, the group and their social background have each a perfectly apportioned share in the composition.

> "FOUR GREAT WALLS IN THE NEW JERUSALEM
> METED ON EACH SIDE BY THE ANGEL'S REED——"

Yes; but to cover such spaces adequately happens even to the greatest artists only once or twice in their career.

V

Marcel Proust

V

Marcel Proust

I

The difficulty of speaking at all adequately of Marcel Proust has grown with the number of volumes of "A la Recherche du Temps Perdu," and also with the lapse of time since the first were published. The cycle, moreover, is still incomplete (though we now know that its conclusion will appear); and the critic who ventures to see a definite intention in the dense and branching pages already published does so at his peril, and on the faith of that sense of inner continuity communicated from the outset by all the greatest novels, from the rambling and extravagant "Gil Blas" to the compact and thrifty "Emma."

The death of Marcel Proust, premature though it was, yet did not happen till his dying hand had put the last words to the last page of his vast narrative. Last words; but unhappily not last touches. The appearance of "La Prisonnière" confirms the report circulated after his death that the volumes then unpublished were left without those innumerable enriching strokes which gave their golden ripeness to the others. But, whether or not these final chapters, written in illness, and clouded (as one perceives from "La Prisonnière") by physical weakness and deep mental distress, fulfil the promise of that unity to which all the strands of the elaborate fabric seem to tend, the first volumes (by which the author's greatness will perhaps finally be measured) make it clear that he himself felt the need of such unity, and would have submitted his restless genius to it if illness had not disintegrated his powers. On this inference the critic will probably have to rest; and it is enough to justify treating the fragment before us as already potentially a whole.

More serious for the critic is the obstacle caused by the long lapse of years since "Du Côté de chez Swann" led off the astounding procession. Since then the conception of the art of fiction, as it had taken shape during the previous half-century, has been unsettled by a series of experiments, each one too promptly heralded as the final and only way of novel-writing. The critics who have handed down these successive ultimata have apparently decided that no interest, even archæological, attaches any longer to the standards and the vocabulary of their predecessors; and this wholesale rejection of past principles has led to a confusion in terms which makes communication difficult and conclusions ambiguous.

An unexpected result of the contradictory clamour
has been to transfer Proust, who ten or twelve years ago
seemed to many an almost unintelligible innovator, back
to his rightful place in the great line of classic tradition. If,
therefore, the attempt to form a judgment of his art has
become doubly arduous it has also become doubly interesting; for Proust, almost alone of his kind, is apparently
still regarded as a great novelist by the innovators, and yet
is already far enough off to make it clear that he was himself that far more substantial thing in the world of art, a
renovator.

With a general knowledge of letters extending far
beyond the usual limits of French culture he combined a
vision peculiarly his own; and he was thus exceptionally
fitted to take the next step forward in a developing art
without disowning its past, or wasting the inherited
wealth of experience. It is as much the lack of general culture as of original vision which makes so many of the
younger novelists, in Europe as in America, attach undue
importance to trifling innovations. Original vision is never
much afraid of using accepted forms; and only the cultivated intelligence escapes the danger of regarding as
intrinsically new what may be a mere superficial change,
or the reversion to a discarded trick of technique.

The more one reads of Proust the more one sees that
his strength is the strength of tradition. All his newest
and most arresting effects have been arrived at through the
old way of selection and design. In the construction of
these vast, leisurely, and purposeful compositions nothing

is really wasted, or brought in at random. If at first Proust seemed so revolutionary it was partly because of his desultory manner and parenthetical syntax, and chiefly because of the shifting of emphasis resulting from his extremely personal sense of values. The points on which Proust lays the greatest stress are often those inmost tremors, waverings, and contradictions which the conventions of fiction have hitherto subordinated to more generalized truths and more rapid effects. Proust bends over them with unwearied attention. No one else has carried as far the analysis of half-conscious states of mind, obscure associations of thought and gelatinous fluctuations of mood; but long and closely as he dwells on them he never loses himself in the submarine jungle in which his lantern gropes. Though he arrives at his object in so roundabout a way, that object is always to report the conscious, purposive conduct of his characters. In this respect he is distinctly to be classed among those whom the jargon of recent philosophy has labelled "behaviourists" because they believe that the proper study of mankind is man's conscious and purposive behaviour rather than its dim unfathomable sources. Proust is in truth the aware and eager inheritor of two great formulas: that of Racine in his psychology, that of Saint-Simon in its anecdotic and discursive illustration. In both respects he is deliberately traditional.

II

Fashions in the arts come and go, and it is of little interest to try to analyze the work of any artist who does not give one the sense of being in some sort above them. In the art of one's contemporaries it is not always easy to say what produces that sense; and perhaps the best way of trying to find out is to apply a familiar touchstone.

Out of all the flux of judgments and theories which have darkened counsel in respect of novel-writing, one stable fact seems always to emerge; the quality the greatest novelists have always had in common is that of making their people live. To ask why this matters more than anything else would lead one into the obscurest mazes of æsthetic; but the fact is generally enough admitted to serve as a ground for discussion. Not all the other graces and virtues combined seem to have in them that aseptic magic. Vivacity, virtuosity, an abundance of episodes, skill in presenting them: what power of survival have these, compared with the sight of the doddering Baron Hulot climbing his stairs to a senile tryst, to Beatrix Esmond descending hers in silver clocks and red-heeled shoes?

M. Jusserand, in his "Literary History of the English People," says of Shakespeare that he was *un grand distributeur de vie,* a great life-giver; it is the very epithet one needs for Proust. His gallery of living figures is immense, almost past reckoning; so far, in that ever-growing throng, it is only the failures that one can count. And Proust's power of evocation extends from the background and middle distance (where some mysterious law of optics seems to make it relatively easy for the novelist to animate his puppets) to that searching "centre front" where his principal characters, so scrutinized, explained, re-explained, pulled about, taken apart and put together again, resist in their tough vitality his perpetual nervous manipulation, and keep carelessly on their predestined way. Swann himself, subjected to so merciless an examination, Swann, as to whose haberdashery, hats, boots, gloves, taste in pictures, books, and women we are informed with an impartial abundance, is never more alive than when, in that terrible scene of the fifth volume, he quietly tells the Duchesse de Guermantes that he cannot promise to go to Italy the following spring with her and the Duke because he happens to be dying. Equally vivid are the invalid aunt in the pale twilight of her provincial bedroom, and the servant Françoise who waits on her, and at her death passes as a matter of course to the rest of the family—amazing composite picture of all the faults and virtues of the old-fashioned French maid-servant. And then there is the hero's grandmother, who fills the pages with a subdued yet tingling vitality from the moment when we first see her dashing out for one of her lonely walks in the rain to that other day, far on in the tale, when, fiercely and doggedly nursed by Françoise, she dies in an equal loneliness; there is the Marquis de Saint-Loup, impetuous, selfish, and sentimental, with his artless veneration for the latest thing in "culture," his snobbishness in the Bohemian world, his simplicity and good-breeding in his own; the Jewish actress, his mistress, who despises him because he is a mere "man of the world" and not one of her own crew of æsthetic charlatans; the great, the abject, the abominable and magnificent Monsieur de Charlus, and the shy scornful Duchesse de Guermantes, with her quickness of wit and obtuseness of heart, her consuming worldliness and her sincere belief that nothing bores her as much as the world—the poor Duchess, mistress of all the social arts, yet utterly nonplussed, and furious, because Swann's announcement that he is dying is made as she is getting into her carriage to go to a big dinner, and nothing in her code teaches her how to behave to a friend tactless enough to blurt out such news at such a moment! Ah, how they all live, and abound each in his or her own sense—and how, each time they reappear (sometimes after disconcertingly long eclipses), they take up their individual rhythm as unerringly as the performers in some great orchestra!

The sense that, through all his desultoriness, Proust always knows whither his people are tending, and which of their words, gestures and thoughts are worth recording; his ease in threading his way through their crowded ranks, fills the reader, from the first, with the feeling of security which only the great artists inspire. Certain novels, beginning very quietly—carelessly, almost—yet convey on the opening page the same feeling of impending fatality as the first bars of the Fifth Symphony. Destiny is knocking at the gate. The next knock may not

THE WRITING OF FICTION

come for a long time; but the reader knows that it *will* come, as surely as Tolstoy's Ivan Ilyitch knew that the mysterious little intermittent pain which used to disappear for days would come back oftener and more insistently till it destroyed him.

There are many ways of conveying this sense of the footfall of Destiny; and nothing shows the quality of the novelist's imagination more clearly than the incidents he singles out to illuminate the course of events and the inner workings of his people's souls. When Imogen, setting forth to meet her adored Posthumus at Milford Haven, asks his servant Pisanio (who has been ordered by the jealous Posthumus to murder her on the way): "How many score of miles may we well ride 'twixt hour and hour?" and, getting the man's anguished answer: "One score 'twixt sun and sun, Madam, 's enough for you, and too much too," exclaims: "*Why, one that rode to's execution, man, could never go so slow——*" or when Gretchen, opening her candid soul to Faust, tells him how she mothered her little sister from the cradle—"My mother was so ill . . . I brought the poor little creature up on milk and water . . . the cradle stood by my bed, she could hardly stir without my waking. I had to feed her, take her into the bed with me, walk the floor with her all night, and be early the next morning at the wash-tub; but I loved her so that I was glad to do it"—when the swift touch of genius darts such rays on the path to come, one is almost tempted to exclaim: There is nothing in mere "situation"—the whole of the novelist's art lies in the

particular way in which he brings the given conjunc-
ture home to the imagination!

Proust had an incredible sureness of touch in shed-
ding this prophetic ray on his characters. Again and again
he finds the poignant word, the significant gesture, as
when, in that matchless first chapter ("Combray") of
"Du Côté de chez Swann" he depicts the suspense of the
lonely little boy (the narrator) who, having been hurried
off to bed without a goodnight kiss because M. Swann is
coming to dine, persuades the reluctant Françoise to
carry to his mother a little note in which he implores
her to come up and see him "about something very
important." So far, the episode is like many in which the
modern novelist has analyzed—especially since "Sinister
Street"—the inarticulate tragedies of childhood. But for
Proust such an episode, in addition to its own significance, has a deeper illuminative use.

"I thought to myself," he goes on, "how Swann would
have laughed at my anguish if he had read my letter, and
guessed its real object" (which was, of course, to get his
mother's goodnight kiss); "but, on the contrary, as I
learned later, for years an anguish of the same kind was the
torture of Swann's own life. That anguish, which consists
in knowing that the being one loves is in some gay scene
[*lieu de plaisir*] where one is not, where there is no hope of
one's being; that anguish, it was through the passion of
love that he experienced it—that passion to which it is in
some sort predestined, to which it peculiarly and specifically pertains"—and then, when Françoise has been per-

suaded to take the child's letter, and his mother (engaged with her guest) does not come, but says curtly: "There is no answer"—"Alas!" the narrator continues, "Swann also had had that experience, had learned that the good intentions of a third person are powerless to move a woman who is irritated at feeling herself pursued in scenes of enjoyment by some one whom she does not love—" and suddenly, by one touch, in the first pages of that quiet opening chapter in which a little boy's drowsy memories reconstitute an old friend's visit to his parents, a light is flashed on the central theme of the book: the hopeless incurable passion of a sensitive man for a stupid uncomprehending woman. The foot-fall of Destiny has echoed through that dull provincial garden, her touch has fallen on the shoulder of the idle man of fashion, and in an instant, and by the most natural of transitions, the quiet picture of family life falls into its place in the great design of the book.

Proust's pages abound in such anticipatory flashes, each one of which would make the fortune of a lesser novelist. A peculiar duality of vision enabled him to lose himself in each episode as it unrolled itself before him— as in this delicious desultory picture of Swann's visit to his old friends—and all the while to keep his hand on the main threads of the design, so that no slightest incident contributing to that design ever escapes him. This degree of saturation in one's subject can be achieved only through something like the slow ripening processes of nature. Tyndall said of the great speculative minds:

"There is in the human intellect a power of expansion—
I might almost call it a power of creation—which is
brought into play by the simple brooding upon facts";
and he might have added that this brooding is one of the
most distinctive attributes of genius, is perhaps as near
an approach as can be made to the definition of genius.

Nothing can be farther from the mechanical ingenu-
ities of "plot"-weaving than this faculty of penetrating
into a chosen subject and bringing to light its inherent
properties. Neither haste to have done, nor fear lest the
reader shall miss his emphasis, ever affects the leisurely
movement of Proust's narrative, or causes him to give
unnatural relief to the passages intended to serve as sign-
posts. A tiny "blaze," here and there, on the bark of one
of the trees in his forest, suffices to show the way; and
the explorer who has not enough wood-craft to discover
these signs had best abstain from the adventure.

III

It was one of the distinctive characters of Proust's genius
that he combined with his great sweep of vision an exquisite delicacy of touch, a solicitous passion for detail. Many
of his pages recall those mediæval manuscripts where the
roving fancy of the scribe has framed some solemn gospel
or epistle in episodes drawn from the life of towns and
fields, or the pagan extravagances of the Bestiary. Jane
Austen never surpassed in conciseness of irony some of

the conversations between Marcel's maiden aunts, or the description of Madame de Cambremer and Madame de Franquetot listening to music; and one must turn to "Cranford" for such microscopic studies of provincial life as that of the bed-ridden aunt, Madame Octave, who is always going to get up the next day, and meanwhile lies beside her bottle of Vichy and her purple velvet prayer-book "bursting with pious images," and listens to Françoise's report of what is going on in the street, down which Madame Goupil, just before a thunder-storm, is seen walking *without her umbrella* in the new silk dress she has made at Châteaudun!

But just as the reader is sinking delectably into the feather-bed of the small town, Proust snatches him up in eagle's talons and swings him over the darkest abysses of passion and intrigue—showing him, in the slow tortures of Swann's love for Odette, and of Saint-Loup's for Rachel, the last depths and involutions of moral anguish, or setting the frivolous careers of the two great Guermantes ladies, the Duchess and the Princess, on a stage vaster than any since Balzac's, and packed with a human comedy as multifarious. This changing but never confusing throng is composed of most of the notable types of a society which still keeps its aristocratic frame-work: the old nobility of the "Faubourg" with their satel-lites; rich and cultivated Jews (such as Swann and Bloch), celebrated painters, novelists, actresses, diplomatists, lawyers, doctors, Academicians; men of fashion and vice, *déclassées* Grand Duchesses, intriguing vulgarians, dowdy great ladies, and all the other figures composing the most various, curious, and restless of modern societies.

Without visible effort Proust's art marshals these throngs and then turns serenely aside to put the last tender touches to his description of the hawthorns at Combray, or the lovely episode of Marcel's first visit to Rachel, where the young man walks up and down under the blossoming pear-trees while Saint-Loup goes to fetch his mistress. Every reader enamoured of the art must brood in amazement over the way in which Proust maintains the balance between these two manners—the broad and the minute. His endowment as a novelist—his range of presentation combined with mastery of his instruments—has probably never been surpassed.

Fascinating as it is to the professional to dwell on this amazing virtuosity, yet the lover of Proust soon comes to feel that his rarest quality lies beyond and above it— lies in the power to reveal, by a single allusion, a word, an image, those depths of soul beyond the soul's own guessing. The man who could write of the death of Marcel's grandmother: "A few hours ago her beautiful hair, just beginning to turn gray . . . had seemed less old than herself. Now, on the contrary, it placed the crown of age on a face grown young again, and from which the wrinkles, the contractions, the heaviness, the tension, the flaccidity caused by suffering had all disappeared. As in the far-off time when her parents had chosen her bridegroom for her, the features of her face were delicately traced in lines of purity and submission, the cheeks shone with chaste hopes, with a dream of bliss, even with an innocent gaiety that the years, one by one, had slowly destroyed. Life, in leaving her had taken with it the disillusionments of life. A smile seemed to rest upon my grandmother's lips. On that funeral bed, death, like the mediæval sculptor, had laid her down in the guise of a young girl—" the man who could find words in which to express the inexpressible emotion with which one comes suddenly, in some apparently unknown landscape, upon a scene long known to the soul (like that mysterious group of trees encountered by Marcel in the course of a drive with Madame de Villeparisis)—the man who could touch with so sure and compassionate a hand on the central mysteries of love and death, deserves at such moments to be ranked with Tolstoy when he describes the death of Prince Andrew, with Shakespeare when he makes Lear say: "Pray you, undo this button. . . ."

IV

Hitherto I have only praised.

In writing of a great creative artist, and especially of one whose work is over, it is always better worth while to dwell on the beauties than to hunt down the blemishes. Where the qualities outweigh the defects the latter lose much of their importance, even when, as sometimes in Proust's case, they are defects in the moral sensibility, that tuning-fork of the novelist's art.

It is vain to deny, or to try to explain away, this particular blemish—deficiency, it should be rather called—in
Proust's work. Undoubtedly there are blind spots in his
books, as there are in Balzac's, in Stendhal's, in Flaubert's;
but Proust's blind spots are peculiarly disconcerting
because they are intermittent. One cannot dismiss the
matter by saying that a whole category of human emotions
is invisible to him, since at certain times his vision is
acutest at the precise angle where the blindness had pre-
viously occurred.

A well-known English critic, confusing the scenes in
which Proust's moral sense has failed him with those (far
more numerous) in which he deliberately portrays the
viler aspects of the human medley, suggests that timo-
rous readers might find unmingled enjoyment in the
perusal of "A la Recherche du Temps Perdu" by the simple expedient of "thinking away" M. de Charlus—as
who should propose "thinking away" Falstaff from the
plays in which he figures! It would, in fact, be almost as
difficult to dismiss M. de Charlus with an "I know thee
not, old man," as Falstaff; and quite as unnecessary. It is
not by daring to do "in the round" a mean or corrupt
character—an Iago, a Lord Steyne, a Philippe Bridau, or
a Valérie Marneffe—that a novelist diminishes the value
of his work. On the contrary, he increases it. Only when
the vileness and the cruelty escape him, when he fails to
see the blackness of the shadow they project, and thus
unconsciously flattens his modelling, does he corre-
spondingly empoverish the picture; and this Proust too
often did—but never in drawing M. de Charlus, whose

ignominy was always as vividly present to him as Iago's or Goneril's to their creator.

There is one deplorable page where the hero and narrator, with whose hyper-sensitiveness a hundred copious and exquisite passages have acquainted us, describes with complacency how he has deliberately hidden himself to spy on an unedifying scene. This episode—and several others marked by the same abrupt lapse of sensibility—might be "thought away" with all the less detriment that, at such moments, Proust's characters invariably lose their *probableness* and begin to stumble through their parts like good actors vainly trying to galvanize a poor play. All through his work there are pages literally trembling with emotion; but wherever the moral sensibility fails, the tremor, the vibration, ceases. When he is unaware of the meanness of an act committed by one of his characters, that character loses by so much of its life-likeness, and, reversing Pygmalion's gesture, the author turns living beings back to stone.

But what are these lapses in a book where countless pages throb with passionate pity and look at one with human eyes? The same man who thus offends at one moment, at the next has one by the heartstrings in a scene such as that where the hero, hearing his grandmother speak for the first time over the telephone, is startled into thoughts of death and separation by the altered sound of a familiar voice; or that in which Saint-Loup comes up to Paris on twenty-four hours' leave, and his adoring mother first exults at the thought that he is going to spend his evening with her, then bitterly divines that he is not, and finally trembles lest, by betraying her disappointment, she shall have spoilt his selfish pleasure. And it is almost always at the very moment when the reader thinks: "Oh, if only he doesn't fail me *now!*" that he floods his squalid scene with the magic of an inexhaustible poetry, so that one could cry out, like Sigmund when the gale blows open the door of the hut: "No one went—some one came! *It is the spring.*"

M. Benjamin Crémieux, whose article on Proust is the most thoughtful study of his work yet published, has come upon the obstacle of Proust's lapses of sensibility, and tried, not very successfully, to turn it. According to this critic, Proust's satire is never "based on a moral ideal," but is always merely "complementary to his psychological analysis. The only occasion" (M. Crémieux continues) "where Proust incidentally speaks of a moral ideal is in the description of the death of Bergotte." He then cites the beautiful passage in question: "Everything happens in our lives as though we had entered upon them with a burden of obligations contracted in an anterior existence; there is nothing in our earthly condition to make us feel that we are under an obligation to be good, to be morally sensitive [*être délicats*], even to be polite; nor, to the artist, to begin over again twenty times a passage which will probably be admired only when his body has been devoured by worms. . . . All these obligations, which have no sanction in our present life, seem to belong to a different world, a world founded on goodness, on moral scruple, on sacrifice, a world entirely different from this one, a world whence we come when we are born on earth, perhaps to return there and live once more under the rule of the unknown laws which we have obeyed here because we carried their principles within ourselves, without knowing who decreed that they should be; those laws to which every deep intellectual labour draws us nearer, and which are invisible only—and not always!—to fools."

It is difficult to see how so deliberate a profession of faith in a moral ideal can be brushed aside as "incidental." The passage quoted would rather seem to be the key to Proust's whole attitude: to its weakness as well as to its strength. For it will be noticed that, among the mysterious "obligations" brought with us from that other "entirely different" world, he omits one; the old stoical quality of courage. That quality, moral or physical, seems never to have been recognized by him as one of the mainsprings of human action. He could conceive of human beings as good, as pitiful, as self-sacrificing, as guided by the most delicate moral scruples; but never, apparently, as brave, either by instinct or through conscious effort.

Fear ruled his moral world: fear of death, fear of love, fear of responsibility, fear of sickness, fear of draughts, fear of fear. It formed the inexorable horizon of his universe and the hard delimitation of his artist's temperament.

In saying so one touches on the narrow margin between the man's genius and his physical disabilities, and at this point criticism must draw back, or linger only in reverent admiration of the great work achieved, the vast register covered, in spite of that limitation, in conflict with those disabilities.

Nietzsche's great saying, "Everything worth while is accomplished notwithstanding" [*trotzdem*], might serve as the epitaph of Proust.